HEBREW CALLIGRAPHY

HEBREW CALLIGRAPHY

A Step-by-Step Guide

JAY SETH GREENSPAN

Schocken Books · New York

Copyright © 1981 by Schocken Books Inc.

All rights reserved under International and Pan-American Copyright Conventions. Published in the United States by Schocken Books Inc., New York. Distributed by Pantheon Books, a division of Random House, Inc., New York.

Library of Congress Cataloging in Publication Data
Greenspan, Jay
  Hebrew calligraphy.
  Bibliography: p.
  Includes index.
  1. Calligraphy, Hebrew.   I. Title.
NK3636.A3G73   745.6′199′24   79-12718

ISBN 0-8052-3720-8 (hardcover)

ISBN 0-8052-0664-7 (paperback)

Designed by Jackie Schuman

Manufactured in the United States of America

9 8 7 6 5

First Schocken Books edition published in 1981

To
my grandparents
Morris and Helen Greenspan
and
Jacob and Meita Haberman
(may their memory be for a blessing)
who planted the seeds

Contents

CONTENTS

Part II / The Plates

CONTENTS

Part IV / The Art of the *Sofer*

Acknowledgments

> Much have I learned from my teachers;
> Even more have I learned from my peers;
> But even more have I learned from my students.
> —*Babylonian Talmud, Ta'anit 7a*

No book is created in a vacuum. I would like to thank all those who had a contribution, large or small, to the writing of this book.

My first teachers—my parents, Philip and Sylvia Greenspan—have given me love and support in all my endeavors. My sister, Sharon, and my brother, Jeffrey, have been there when I needed help. And the members of my extended family have always surrounded me with warmth and love.

Without Mark Loeb, who taught me what calligraphy is, and without David Moss, who taught me by example, I would not be a calligrapher today.

Special thanks are due my friends Zev Shanken and Lynn Ellenson. Without their encouragement and prodding at and from the very beginning, this book would never have been attempted.

Penny Perry, Angela Konishi, and Judith Netterstrom Martens have always helped me, each in her own unique way, through difficult times; I prize their love and friendship.

I would like to thank many people at Schocken Books: Eva Glaser, who initiated the project, first, for her enthusiasm, then for her patience; Seymour Barofsky, for advice and editing of the manuscript in its early stages; Arthur H. Samuelson, for his patience and prodding; and Patricia Woodruff for help and the answers to my questions. Finally,

ACKNOWLEDGMENTS

I want to acknowledge the extraordinary time and care Millicent Fairhurst has devoted to the production of this book.

I especially thank Karen Ready for the immense effort she gave to the final editing of the manuscript.

I owe a unique debt to Dr. David Steinberg and the Lahey Clinic in Boston.

I am grateful for the support of the members of the New York Havurah, and the students, teachers, and parents of the Havurah School.

Only through teaching and answering the countless questions of my students (at the 92nd Street YM-YWHA and the Park Avenue Synagogue) have I gained the practical knowledge for this book; I thank all my students, past, present, and future.

While I may urge my students to strive for perfection, and may aim for it myself, I make many mistakes; I ask understanding of those whom I have not acknowledged because I may not have been conscious of your contribution.

And finally to one special person: Set me as a seal upon your heart:

> Gather this from hand of mine
> for love so deeply given
> Remember my touch and lips upon your eyes
> till I return to you by and by

J.S.G.

Introduction

The Hebrew language is over three thousand years old. The earliest Hebrew letter forms were borrowed from the Phoenician, about 1100 B.C.E. (Before Common Era), and were highly pictographic. For example, ꓶ (*gimmel*) looks like the hump of a *gamal*, a camel. ꓹ (*mem*) is a representation of running water; it is an impression of *mayim,* water. ○ (*ayin*) pictures an *ayin,* an eye. w (*shin*) looks like a *shin,* a tooth. This Phoenician alphabet can be seen in the chart (figure 1) on p. xiv.

Development of the Hebrew letters into forms similar to those we know today occurred around the time of the destruction of the second Temple, during the Roman occupation of Judea, around 70 C.E. (Common Era). Coins found at Masada—the last stronghold of the Jewish revolt against the Romans—contain two types of lettering. One might be called the ancient style; the other might be easily recognizable as the early precursor of the Hebrew letters of today. Since both types of letters appear on these coins, as well as on different documents from this same period, scholars believe this was a transitional period for the development of Hebrew letters. Documents like the Dead Sea Scrolls show what might be called "modern" letters that are highly recognizable to a contemporary reader.

Hebrew, like most languages, is made up of consonants and vowels. There are twenty-two letters, five of which have "final forms," used when those letters appear at the end of a word. All the letters in Hebrew are consonants. The vowels, except for four, are represented by dots and dashes that are placed under the letters (and in one case, above). See the Hebrew alphabet chart on p. xiv, and the vowel chart (figure 2) on p. xv.

Name [a]	Type[b]	Basic Script[c]	Block[d]	Cursive[e]	Phoeni-cian[f]	Sound[g]	Numerical Value[h]
alef	א	א	×	k	ꓘ	'	1
vet(bet)[#]	בּ ב	בּ ב	ב	ə	ꓩ	v(b)[#]	2
gimmel	ג	ג	ג	ɕ	1	g	3
dalet	ד	ד	ד	3	◁	d	4
he	ה	ה	ה	כ	⅁	h	5
vav	ו	ו	ו	I	Y	v	6
zayin	ז	ז	ז	ȝ	I	z	7
het	ח	ח	ח	ɳ	目	h	8
tet	ט	ט	v	6	⊕	t	9
yod	י	י	י	'	Z	y	10
khaf(kaf)[#]	*כנךּ	*פ ךּך	*כ ך	*כף	ꓦ	kh(k)[#]	20
lamed	ל	ל	ל	ꝭ	ᒪ	l	30
mem	*ם ם	*ם ם	*ם ם	*פא	⅄	m	40
nun	*נ ן	*י ן	*נ ן	*ן	Ꝺ	n	50
samekh	ס	ס	ס	ο	Ŧ	s	60
ayin	ע	ע	ע	y	O	'	70
fe(pe)[#]	*ם פ ף	*פפף	*פ ף	*ℓℓə	⅂	f(p)[#]	80
tzaddi	*צ ץ	*צ ץ	*צ ץ	*ℓȝ	ᴦ	tz	90
kof	ק	ק	ק	ρ	Φ	k	100
resh	ר	ר	ר	כ	ꝯ	r	200
shin(sin)[o]	שׁ שׂ	שׁ שׂ	ꓦ	ℓ	W	sh(s)[o]	300
tav	ת	ת	ת	♪	+	t	400

Fig. 1. Hebrew alphabet chart.

*This is the final form (*sofit* in Hebrew). These are the five letters that assume special

[xiv]

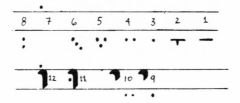

Fig. 2. Vowel Chart. Each vowel in this list is given its name and then its sound. (The sounds are only approximate.) 1) *Patah—ah.* 2) *Kamatz—ah* or *aw.* 3) *Hirik—ih.* 4) *Tzereh—*between *ay* and *eh.* 5) *Sehgol—eh.* 6) *Koobootz—*between *ooh* and *uh.* 7) *Holem—oh.* 8) *Sh'va—*silent. 9) *Hirik—ee.* 10) *Tzereh—ay.* 11) *Shoorook—ooh.* 12) *Holem—oh.*

Hebrew is read and written from right to left, the opposite of English. When the Greeks adopted the Phoenician alphabet, they began to write their documents in two directions. The first line read the Phoenician way, from right to left. To read the second line, the reader would drop down from the last letter of the first line to the letter directly below it, and then begin reading from left to right. At the end (at the right) of this line, the reader dropped to the third line and began reading from right to left again. Reading a document like this would look like it does in figure 3. This way of writing and reading became very confusing, and eventually was standardized so that all lines read from left to right, which is how we read and write English.

forms at the end of a word. When these letters appear at the beginning or middle of a word, they appear in their other form.

\# Many letters may appear with a dot called a *dagesh* inside, but this affects their name and sound in only three letters, as indicated by the names and sounds in parentheses. *Vet* with a dot becomes *bet; khaf* becomes *kaf;* and *fe* becomes *pe.*

° The letter *shin* is indicated by a dot in its upper right-hand corner; the letter *sin* is indicated by a dot in its upper left-hand corner.

ᵃ The transliteration of the names of the Hebrew letters is based on that used in the *Encyclopaedia Judaica,* and will be used throughout the book. There are other ways of transliterating the letters. Hebrew letters are used in at least four languages: Hebrew, Aramaic, Judeizmo (often called Ladino), and Yiddish. Each has a slightly different orthography.

ᵇ This type face is the most frequently used in many Hebrew books, and probably the most recognizable, and so is used as a standard of comparison.

ᶜ This is the basic script taught in the plates.

ᵈ These are stick letters which can be used in block printing.

ᵉ Most writers of Hebrew use this script for everyday writing. Note that there are two ways of writing *fe sofit.*

ᶠ These ancient letter forms (dating from around 1100 B.C.E.) are the ancestors of early Hebrew letters.

ᵍ These are the approximate sounds that each letter stands for. Two letters, both indicated by *',* are silent. They are *alef* and *ayin* (though some Hebrew speakers pronounce *ayin* almost like a gulping sound, at the back of the throat). The sound *kh* is similar to the "ch" in the Scots word "loch." The *h* is very similar (though some Hebrew speakers pronounce *het* almost like a choking sound, at the back of the throat).

ʰ Each letter has a numerical value. Numbers are almost always written using letters that are their equivalents.

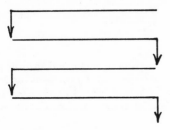

Fig. 3. Early writing and reading by the Greeks.

Occasionally, words are abbreviated. When single words are abbreviated, a single mark (like an apostrophe) is added at the end of the abbreviated word, as in the following examples. יִשְׂרָאֵל [*yisrael,* Israel] is abbreviated יִשְׂרַ׳. שֶׁבַּתּוֹרָה [*shebatorah,* that which is in the Torah] is abbreviated שֶׁבַּתּ׳. An important example is God's name. God's name is considered holy, and can be written in many different ways. To avoid profaning God's name, it is almost always abbreviated (except in sacred documents) as הַ׳ [הַשֵּׁם, which stands for *hashem,* The Name]. The mark at the end of each word stands for the letter or letters missing.

When acronyms are written, two marks are placed between the last two letters. זַצַ״ל (read *zatzal*) stands for זֵכֶר צַדִּיק לִבְרָכָה [*zekher tzaddik livrakha,* may the memory of the righteous be for a blessing]. רַמְבַּ״ם (pronounced *rambam*) stands for רַבִּי מֹשֶׁה בֶּן מַיְמוֹן [*rabi moshe ben maimon,* Maimonides—often called Rambam]. תַּנַ״ך (read *tanakh*) stands for תּוֹרָה נְבִיאִים כְּתוּבִים [*torah, n'veeim, k'tuvim,* Torah, Prophets, Writings—the three divisions of the Bible (Old Testament only)]. עַ״ש can stand for עַיֵן שָׁם [*ayain sham,* ibid.] or עֶרֶב שַׁבָּת [*erev shabbat,* the eve of the Sabbath], depending upon the context in which it appears.

But Hebrew, the language of the Bible (Old Testament), is more than an alphabet. It's a language whose very essence is holiness. The letter *yod*—the first letter you will learn as a student of Hebrew calligraphy—is also the first letter in God's name. And essentially, all Hebrew letters contain a *yod* as part of their structure. To the kabbalists—the Jewish mystics—Hebrew letters had great power, and elaborate permutations of letters were devised for all kinds of mystical speculation.

Hebrew letters also have numerical values (as can be seen in the chart on p. xiv), and have additive value when written together. When single-digit numbers are written, a mark (like the one used in single abbreviated words) follows the letter. 'ﬤ is three; 'ז is seven. Complex numbers are written combining letters and placing two marks (like those used in acronyms) between the last two letters. 32 is written ל"ב (30 + 2). 65 is written ס"ה (60 + 5). 741 is written תשמ"א (400 + 300 + 40 + 1). This number can also stand for the Jewish calendar year 5741. The 1000's are often deleted when writing the year, but sometimes they are indicated by using an oversize letter representing the number of 1000's. So 5741 is sometimes written ה̇תשמ"א. Two special combinations are used for 15 and 16, written ט"ו (9 + 6) and ט"ז (9 + 7), because the usual combinations (10 + 5 and 10 + 6) represent forms of God's name.

Not only are numbers represented by letters, but words also can have numerical values. Jews throughout the centuries have practiced *gematria;* that is, they ascribe significant meaning to the numerical values of words. For example, certain words are the numerical equivalents of others. The word אריה [*aryeh,* lion] has a value of 216 (1 + 200 + 10 + 5) and is the numerical equivalent of גבורה [*g'voorah,* strength]. Rabbis (and others) throughout the generations have composed a great deal of midrashic material* using *gematria* to explore the meanings of texts. In the Yiddish Warsaw Troupe's powerful film version (1932) of S. An-ski's play *The Dybbuk,* the young protagonist, Chonon, uses kabbalistic formulas to help attain his goal of marrying Leah. He begins by calculating the numerical value of her name (לאה is 36—30 + 1 + 5), and then begins to speculate on equivalents to gain the power he needs.

Once you begin to practice forming Hebrew letters, you will see that they have an internal power all their own. Each letter has its own beauty, its own sense of proportion, its own meaning. There's the ascendancy of the *lamed,* the compactness of the *yod,* the roundness of the *shin,* the openness of the *vet.* Many *midrashim,* old and modern, have been written about letters and their powers. Ben Shahn's *The Alphabet of Creation* is an adaptation of an old *midrash.* Lawrence

---

* A *midrash* (pl. *midrashim*) is any sort of homiletical material, often using symbolism, metaphor, analogy, poetry, alliteration, onomatopoeia, and other literary devices to express a thought, often related to the Bible, or based upon Biblical verses. There are other ways to define *midrash.*

Kushner explores both traditional and contemporary *midrashim* in *The Book of Letters: A Mystical Alef-bait.* And Mark Podwal, in *A Book of Hebrew Letters,* explores the alphabet through drawings that act as visual *midrashim.*

Since representational art is forbidden by the Torah, Jews developed very few crafts.* Since books (more accurately, scrolls) were central to Jewish life from the very beginning, concentration on the accuracy and consistency of letters and words became paramount. The reverence in which the Jews have held books has led to the phrase "the people of the book" becoming an apt synonym for the Jews. And the *sofer*—literally, "the writer"—became central to this preoccupation and developed his craft to a high technical and spiritual art.

Learning to form letters beautifully—learning the art of calligraphy—is a process that may bring you many insights about yourself and the world around you.

The physical preparation involves the kind of relaxation that will enable you to use your body as a tool (and the calligraphic equipment as extensions of that) and let the pen flow to form letters of beauty and grace.

The spiritual connection—as the ancient scribes and the kabbalists knew and traditional *sofrim* still experience—is already contained in the alphabet; you have only to begin to study the letters to allow them to make this connection. You needn't even have any prior knowledge of Hebrew. In making the letters you will become intimately involved in each letter. You will learn to recognize every unique part that distinguishes one from the other. You will learn the beauty, power, and majesty the letters have, and appreciate each one for its own sake.

The deeper you delve, the more you may discover: Echoes of the *midrash* that the first Torah, created before God created the world, was written in black fire on white fire. Echoes of the letters incised all the way through the stone by the hand of God at Mount Sinai. Echoes of Ezra "the Scribe" rededicating the people to the Torah after their re-

* It is stated in Exodus 20:4 and in Deuteronomy 5:8: "You shall not make for yourself a sculptured image, or any likeness of what is in the heavens above, or on the earth below, or in the waters under the earth." (Translation from *The Torah: The Five Books of Moses* [Philadelphia: Jewish Publication Society, 1962], pp. 134 and 334.) This commandment was interpreted by the Rabbis to extend to all forms of art. Though acceptance of this prohibition has diminished slowly throughout the millennia, it held strong influence over the early development (or lack of such development) of art and craft among Jews. In early times, only in a few areas such as the *sofer*'s art and in the construction of the Tabernacle and the Temple did true craft find its expression.

turn from the Babylonian captivity and thus insuring Jewish survival. Echoes of Rabbi Hanania's martyrdom, wrapped in a Torah and set afire, declaring: "The parchment is burning, but the letters are flying free." Echoes of the beautiful Hebrew manuscripts produced by medieval Jewish scribes. Echo after echo after echo. . . .

When I do calligraphy I hear some of these echoes, and other, more personal ones. For me, calligraphy is often a meditative activity. I meditate on my past and my present. Sometimes I may think about my grandparents and the warm and loving Jewish consciousness they gave to my childhood. Sometimes I may think about my parents, my brother and sister, my extended family. Sometimes I may think about the more ordinary things that make up daily life, shopping, cooking, making phone calls. And sometimes I may think about life and personal feelings of sadness, happiness, love. It isn't only when writing letters that such things happen, but often (though not always) the activity of lettering allows my mind to explore myself, my thoughts, feelings, and experiences.

To seek out these and other dimensions—your own personal and unique ones—when you do calligraphy, you must take aim at a certain center within you and see each letter with a concentration that allows your inner "eye" and inner "hand" to guide your eye and hand. I could draw an analogy from a little book called *Zen in the Art of Archery.** When the Zen archer aims his arrow at a target, his aim is not for some faraway goal; his aim is to hit the mark within himself. The inner aiming is the crucial and real one; it must take place before a perfect shot. The archer even aims with his eye closed. No external target can ever be hit if the internal center is not aimed for first. This is what you must strive for. To hit the mark of perfection in Hebrew lettering, to really "see" the letter, to really understand not only the structural processes involved in forming a letter, but also the highly individualized force calligraphy has on each one of us, you must aim for the perfect letters within. Only then will you hit the target. (And only after the discipline of practice will you begin to develop creative expression for the skill you have studied.)

Now you are ready to begin your first step. When children began their first day of *ḥeder* (one-room religious instruction) in Eastern Europe (until the Holocaust destroyed Jewish life there), they first learned the alphabet. The *melamed* (instructor) would put honey on the slates

* Eugen Herrigel, *Zen in the Art of Archery* (New York: Vintage Books, 1971).

on which the letters were written. The children would then lick the honey from the slates, and their first "taṣte" of letters would then be "sweet in their mouths." May your first taste, and every taste, be sweet, and full of joy!

Jay Seth Greenspan

New York, March 1980
Adar 5740

I

PRELIMINARIES AND PREPARATION

1
What You Need

WORK SPACE AND LIGHTING

To begin with, set aside a single area where you will regularly work and practice calligraphy. You may simply designate a certain table at first, and keep all your tools and materials in a drawer or box. Later, when you are ready to begin more advanced work, a drafting table and special storage space may become necessary. The surface you write on must be square or rectangular, not round or oval. It should also be smooth (free of bumps) and relatively stable, not wobbly. A small drafting board that can be propped up on a table may be a good investment. Some calligraphers recommend a slanted surface for writing. It certainly is easier on the back! If you desire a slanted surface, take a small drafting board and place a book or two under it so that it slants toward you. Of course, you can use whatever flat surface is handy.

If you are right-handed, the light should come from the upper left-hand corner of your work area. If you are left-handed, light should come from the upper right-hand corner. In either case, it is important to use good lighting. Do not rely upon overhead lighting. It is usually not specific enough nor strong enough to keep the shadow of your

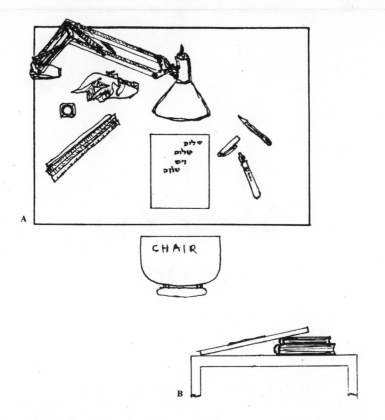

Fig. 4. a) Work table and spring lamp (top view). b)Drafting board propped up by books (side view).

hand from falling over your work. At first, you may be satisfied with a table lamp. Soon, however, you may wish to have a spring lamp that clamps onto the side of your work table. The advantages of a spring lamp are that you can move it and its light can be focused. Use a strong bulb, and fluorescent lighting if you wish, though I find it too harsh and cold. (See figure 4.)

MATERIALS

Here are all the materials you will need for calligraphy (except for the pen and nib, which will be taken up next).

STRAIGHT EDGE
Any good straight edge is usable, although a ruler is preferred. Make

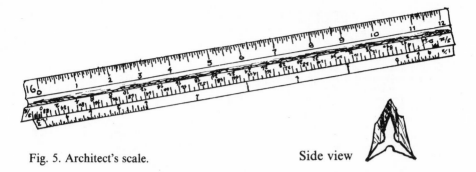

Fig. 5. Architect's scale.   Side view

sure it is accurate (metal or plastic or wood are all fine). An architect's scale (see figure 5) is most useful in more advanced projects. Be careful not to buy an engineer's scale, which is similarly shaped.

PENCIL
Pencils range from hard to soft and are graded accordingly. H stands for hard, B for soft. A 9H pencil is very hard, an 8H a little less hard, and so on. A 6B pencil is very soft, a 5B a little less soft, and so forth. I recommend an HB pencil (see figure 6). The combination of letters indicates that it is a medium-hard pencil (approximately equivalent to a No. 2 pencil.) You should have several sharpened pencils available at your work space at all times. A good manual or electric pencil sharpener for your table would be a worthwhile investment.

Fig. 6. HB pencil.

PAPER
It is possible to write on any surface, from tissue to watercolor paper, though the former is extremely porous and the latter quite bumpy. Though some teachers recommend bond paper for the purposes of learning calligraphy, I recommend graph paper that is ruled ten squares to the inch (see figure 7). (Why I have chosen ten squares per inch will become apparent in the section on "Angles," p. 29.) Graph

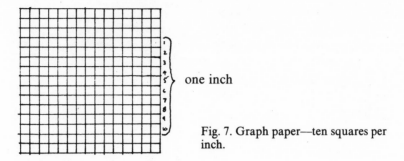

one inch

Fig. 7. Graph paper—ten squares per inch.

paper provides the beginner with horizontal and vertical cues that help determine letter proportion.

RAGS

The rag you use to clean your pen or wipe off surplus ink must not be so absorbent that it takes off all the ink, nor must it be so *un*absorbent that it removes little or no ink. Diapers, paper towels, tissues, etc., are too absorbent. Rags made from 100 percent synthetic material are insufficiently absorbent. Do not use rags that are too thick or full of loose threads, for they will catch on your pen nib and smear letters. The best rags are those made from a blend of cotton and synthetic fiber, such as sheets and pillowcases.

A blotter is not recommended at this early stage. It may prove useful later, when illumination techniques are taken up.

INK

There are two kinds of ink, waterproof and nonwaterproof. Waterproof ink is most suitable for dip pens. Waterproof ink contains lacquers that make it impervious to water; that is, water will not affect the

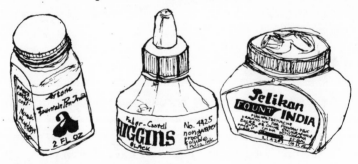

Fig. 8. Three choices for non-waterproof ink.

ink once it has dried. This also means that ink can dry in your fountain pen, and harden and clog (and possibly corrode) the nib and barrel. The only way to clean or remove waterproof ink is by using special detergent liquids, which may further damage a fountain pen. All this leads me to conclude that you should use nonwaterproof ink (see figure 8) in fountain pens. Using nonwaterproof ink means that you will be able to clean your pen fairly easily by just rinsing it under running water, and flushing water in and out of the chamber until the water runs clear. (See the section on "Care of Pen and Nib," p. 15.) Nonwaterproof does not necessarily mean that the ink will wash off your clothes well.

There are many brands of nonwaterproof ink on the market, including Artone Fountain Pen India Ink, Higgins Non-Waterproof Black, Winsor & Newton Liquid India, Pelikan Fount India, Osmiroid Ink, Stephen's Calligraph Ink, and the Pelikan "4000" series. (I prefer Artone or Higgins, though you might find some of the others more suitable to your needs.)

In reading the information that comes with most fountain pens you will notice that it probably contains the warning not to use India inks. The term "India ink" refers to waterproof black ink. There are also nonwaterproof India inks.

The same principle, nonwaterproof versus waterproof, applies to colored inks. Most colored inks are waterproof. So when I want to write something in a color other than black, I use bottled watercolors, i.e., those already in liquid form. There are also some nonwaterproof colored inks, and Artone makes a Sepia Fount that is a rich reddish-brown color.

Let me add one more proviso. Once you decide to use black ink in a pen, stay with black for that pen and set of nibs. No matter how well you wash out the pen and nibs and chamber, you will never be able to get the carbon (which makes the ink black) out completely. So I suggest you keep one pen and set of nibs for black, another pen and set of nibs for all colored inks, washing your pen and nibs out between each color. Of course, you can always convert a pen used for colored ink to one for black, but not vice versa.

Finally, there is a useful rule I have in my classes: Keep your ink capped tightly. The most dangerous bottle of ink is one that is lightly capped. At some point you may reach for the bottle without thinking, only to see streams and splotches appear on the manuscript you have been working on for hours. (For the same reason, keep the bottle away from your elbows and forearms.)

PENS

Although one might justify the use of any writing instrument for doing lettering, for the purposes of this book it is necessary that the pen be a broad-nibbed pen. This means that ball-point pens and other writing

Fig. 9. Quills and dip pens. a) Goose quill. b) Turkey quill. c) Speedball. d) Mitchell. e) Crow quill.

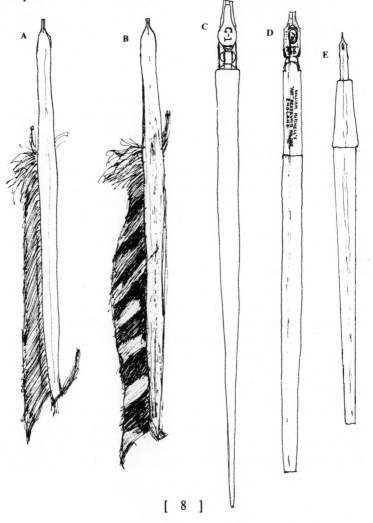

instruments (pencils, felt-tip markers, etc.) should not be used for these alphabets. There are now several brands of felt-tip markers that approximate the broad nib in their design. One of these is Eberhard Faber DeSiGN STRIPE Chisel Point 492. While they are useful and can perform the same function as a metal nib, they are not as durable, nor as precise.

The earliest pens were reeds. Quills cut from geese, turkeys, or even porcupines were also used, and are still used today. Most *sofrim*—Hebrew scribes—use either turkey or goose quills for their work. There is also a manmade quill called the Braun (Embouchure) Quill. Made of plastic, it nicely approximates the feel of a real quill. (See figure 9.)

Today a wide variety of pens is available, from dip pens (such as those made by Mitchell and Speedball) to good fountain pens (Osmiroid, Platignum, Pelikan 120, MontBlanc, etc.) (See figure 10.) Osmiroid makes two pens suitable for calligraphy. The Osmiroid 65 has a thicker barrel; it fills with a lever mechanism. The Osmiroid 75, which is a little more expensive, fills with a screw-type plunger mechanism. For most of my work, I use the Osmiroid 65, but I use it as a dip pen. It holds a good deal of ink when dipped. I use the 75 as a fountain pen. (See the section on "Priming the Pen" on page 14.)

The Platignum is of equally good quality, though I find its filling technique a bit awkward, and its nib does not give the same feather-thin lines as the Osmiroid. I would also recommend the Pelikan 120, though it only offers three sizes of nibs, and is more expensive than Osmiroid or Platignum.

DIP PENS

Dip pens consist of a simple nib that fits into a separate holder. You must dip your pen in ink frequently. Some have built-in or removable reservoirs to hold ink, but in fact they hold relatively little. Beginners may find that the pen is heavily laden with ink at first, but by the fourth or fifth stroke has almost none left. It may take a good while for the beginning student to master the art of handling this difficulty. It is because of this that I recommend fountain pens for the beginner.

Fountain pens usually supply the nib with a consistent, smooth, long-lasting supply of ink, enabling you to write long lines of letters before you have to refill (or dip your pen, if you are using a fountain pen in this way, as I recommend in the case of the Osmiroid 65). I want to state emphatically, however, that I myself often use dip pens and

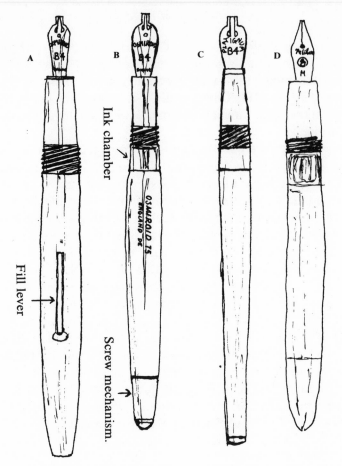

Fig. 10. a) Osmiroid "65." b) Osmiroid "75." c) Platignum. d) Pelikan 120.

their ancestors, quills, especially when working on parchment or using special inks that might clog a fountain pen, such as *sofer*'s ink, Chinese stick ink, or gold ink. Dip pens (such as Mitchell) often give sharper, more clearly defined letters. They are also useful for making large letters, as the dip pen nibs are available in a much greater range of widths than are fountain pen nibs.

NIBS

If you look at any set of pens in an art supply store, especially dip pens, you will see that the nibs come in a variety of shapes and sizes (see figure 11). A broad nib is one that appears very wide when viewed from the top but when viewed from the side appears thin. This allows you to vary the thickness of a stroke simply by moving the nib in different directions on the paper as you write. It is this differentiation of stroke width that defines the kind of calligraphic lettering we will be learning.

Broad nibs have various names, depending upon the type of pen you are using. Broad-nibbed Mitchell pens are available in three series, Italic, Round Hand, and Poster; there are twelve Round Hand nibs, differentiated by width according to number, ranging from 0 to 6, 0

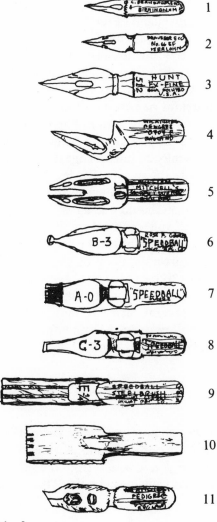

Fig. 11. Nibs. 1), 2), 3) Fine and extra–fine points. 4) Elbow point. 5) "Scroll writer." 6) Speedball "B" series (circular tip). 7) Speedball "C" series (square tip). 8) Speedball "C" series (broad nib). 9) Speedball steel brush. 10) Coit pen point. 11) Mitchell Round Hand point, oblique (for left–handed writers).

being the widest. (The Italic series are narrower nibs, the Poster series broader.) For Speedball pens broad nibs are available in the "C" series. C-O is the widest, C-6 the narrowest. In the Osmiroid fountain pen line, the widest nib is B-4, and the nibs decrease in width by the following designations: B-3, B-2, Broad Straight, Medium Straight, Fine Intermediate Straight, Fine Straight, Extra Fine Straight. The Platignum follows the same system of designation, with one nib not included in its series—the Fine Intermediate Straight. The Pelikan 120 and MontBlanc both take only three nibs: Medium, Fine, and Extra Fine.

It is important that the nib has the ability to make a differentiated stroke, that is, wide by movement of the pen in one direction and thin by movement of the pen in a different direction. B-4 nibs are the widest ones available for the fountain pens, and therefore I recommend this size nib for beginners, since the bigger the scale in which you work, the easier it is for you to see what you are doing, and the easier to discern mistakes. (Using the B-4 nib effectively limits your choice of fountain pen to the Osmiroid 65, Osmiroid 75, or Platignum. Much later you may wish to buy narrower nibs when you feel ready to scale down the size of your letters.) While nibs from different brands of dip pens may be interchangeable, each brand of fountain pens has its own set of nibs specifically designed for that brand of pen, and nibs made for one brand do not fit the barrels of another brand.

If you should find a new nib to be "scratchy" when you write with it, see if you can't return it in exchange for a smoother nib. If not, "scratchy" nibs can be smoothened by stroking the nib a few times in one direction along its edge on a "crocus" cloth, a very fine abrasive paper like emery cloth, available at hardware or art supply stores. Because of this potential difficulty, take the time when buying a pen to test several nibs (without ink) on paper and on your fingertip for smoothness. At the same time, check the nib to make sure none of the three prongs is bent.

PUTTING PEN AND NIB TOGETHER

Okay, so now you have a B-4 nib (see figures 12 and 13). Take a look at it! Notice that the nib is wide if you look at it from the top, but very thin if you look at it from the side or edge. Also notice that the B-4 nib has two slits near its tip. These help the flow of ink and keep it uni-

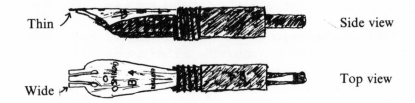

Thin ↗   Side view

Wide ↗   Top view

Fig. 12. Osmiroid B–4 nib.

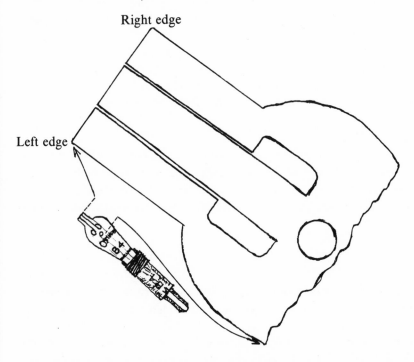

Fig. 13. Enlarged view of part of Osmiroid B–4 nib, showing right and left edges. (Entire nib shown is actual size.)

form. It is very important to keep the *entire* edge of the nib on the paper when writing and apply *even* pressure to both right and left sides of the nib (see figure 21 on p. 21). You will find then that your strokes are evenly made and the edges are sharp. You will also find that, if you apply too much pressure to either side of the nib—by pressing too hard with your thumb, for example—you will eventually bend one of the three "fingers," or prongs, of the nib. You should try to create a tripodal effect between your thumb, forefinger, and middle finger. The

[13   ]

thumb and forefinger press down evenly on the nib, while the middle finger counterbalances this with a reverse pressure. The important thing to realize is that the nib can withstand a great deal of *even* lateral pressure, but it does not deal well with torque (i.e., twisting, or uneven pressure.)

Before you can use a new nib, you'll need to wash off the oily film the manufacturer puts there to protect the nib, as it also keeps the nib from accepting ink. The best solvent, I have found, is saliva. Place a drop of saliva on your finger and wash the nib, then wipe it with your rag.

In putting nib and pen barrel together, in order to prevent harmful twisting of the point, hold the nib stationary between thumb and forefinger and screw the barrel onto the nib. Do not tighten the nib too much. When you feel resistance, stop turning the barrel.

FILLING THE PEN

Before uncapping the ink bottle, shake it lightly. This insures even suspension if it has been standing for some time. When the bubbles subside, open the bottle, being careful not to be caught and splattered by a bursting ink bubble. Fill the pen carefully, according to the manufacturer's instructions.

PRIMING THE PEN

Once you have filled the pen with ink, or merely dipped it, you are ready to prime the pen to get the ink flowing. To prime the pen, hold it evenly balanced between thumb and forefinger and rest it on your

Fig. 14. Priming the pen. Move the pen on its edge (1), then downward (2), applying even lateral pressure at all times.

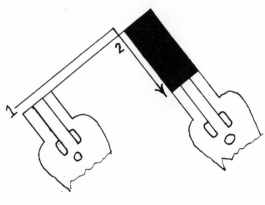

middle finger (see section on "How to Hold the Pen" on page 19). Applying even lateral pressure, move the pen entirely on its edge. What results is a thin line. Then move the pen downward using the broadness of the nib (see figure 14). Friction of the nib along the surface of the paper and the combined motion of these two movements should draw ink. If this does not succeed, previously used ink may have dried on the nib, and it should be wiped off with your rag using the pinching procedure (described in the next section "Care of the Pen and Nib"). In pens that have screw-type plunger filling mechanisms, such as the Osmiroid 75 or Pelikan 120, vacuum may also hold the ink back by counteracting the friction of the nib along the surface of the paper. Release the screw plunger a tiny bit to start the ink flowing and then wipe the nib clean again.

CARE OF THE PEN AND NIB
Each time you dip your pen into ink, including filling, wipe off any excess ink from the nib by taking several thicknesses of rag between your thumb and forefinger and pinching the nib while moving the pen away. This will prevent excess ink drying on the nib and thereby impeding the flow of ink. If after a while you notice that the top of your nib is covered with dried ink, it means you have not wiped your nib carefully enough. Every time you stop writing, the ink flow is suspended and ink on the nib may begin evaporating and drying. To get the ink flowing again, wipe the nib and repeat the priming procedure.

After a certain time, depending upon how frequently you use the pen, it will be advisable to clean your nib and pen barrel. To clean the nib, first remove it from the barrel by holding the nib and unscrewing the barrel. If you find that the nib resists easy removal (because of too much dried, hardened ink at the juncture of nib and barrel), place the pen under warm—not hot—running water, and carefully apply turning pressure until the dried ink loosens and the barrel and nib can be separated. Once the nib is removed, drop it in a jar of cold water overnight, letting it soak until all the ink has dissolved. Rinse it thoroughly and dry it well before using it again. To clean the barrel (and this should be done whether or not you fill your pen), hold the open end of the barrel under cool running water. Then, using the filling mechanism, flush water in and out of the chamber until the water runs clear. Shake out excess water and insert the corner of a facial tissue into the chamber to dry it, twisting it as you move it into the barrel.

2

Preparing Yourself for Calligraphy

DISCIPLINE, SPEED, AND UNDERSTANDING

The more you understand before you start writing, the more you will learn. Do not push yourself beyond the present moment's task; concentrate only upon the stroke at hand. Relax. Do deep breathing so that your body pace is slow. Try to write with your eyes closed so that you can incorporate new elements into your inner eye and let that guide your hand. You must remember that you are learning a new skill. Have patience. Things may be awkward and difficult at first. Your progress may not be as fast as you expect. The more carefully you learn fundamentals correctly, the better will they be integrated into your later learning.

Our bodies are also tools for calligraphy. So good posture is essential. Put your paper straight in front of you (except for the left-handed; see page 21 for instructions). Sit straight, with your feet flat on the floor. Place your hands in a triangle in front of you, centered in front of your nose and equidistant from the right and left shoulders. This will place them in a plane that runs through the center of your body (through the spine), dividing your body in half. This will give you the optimum distance for writing (see figure 15). You should write at this

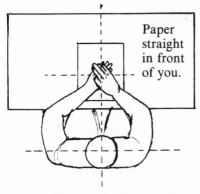

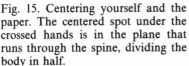

Fig. 15. Centering yourself and the paper. The centered spot under the crossed hands is in the plane that runs through the spine, dividing the body in half.

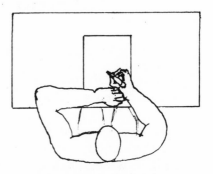

Fig. 16. Position of arms when writing. The right hand is positioned so that the edge of the nib is at the centered spot; the left hand is placed at the bottom of the sheet for balance.

same centered spot at all times. If you want to write in the lower left-hand corner of your paper, move the paper to this centered spot. If you want to write in the upper right-hand corner of the paper, move it to the same centered spot. You may move your hand away from the center spot after writing every two or three letters, but then move hand and paper back to center spot. If you are right-handed, use your left arm for balance, holding it near the edge of the table close to you, leaning along the length of that edge (see figure 16). Left-handed people will also have an optimum spot, but its position will depend on how they hold the pen (see "Notes for the Left-handed" on page 21).

PLACEMENT OF THE BODY

You should be as close as possible to the work you are doing, so as to become involved in it, and to increase your concentration on the material at hand, especially the smallest area that you are working on. Concentrate on the single leaf on the individual branch of the tree of the forest. Being close enables you to see clearly each element and stroke. It makes concentration and the imprint on the mind's eye much stronger. So sit as close as you can to the table, with feet flat on the floor, body relaxed. If you use a flat table, it will be a little easier on the back and shoulders to lean forward slightly.

PAPER PLACEMENT

Place the paper (if you are right-handed; see page 21 for the left-handed) centered in front of you and straight, not slanting either to the right or to the left (see figure 15). The bottom of the paper should be parallel to the edge of the table. You may place the paper vertically or horizontally. This nonslanted placement insures two things: It gives you the same perspective each time you write, without the danger of changing a slant by a few degrees each time the paper is moved. And you will be writing the way you read.

It is also always a good idea to write on a pad, or at least several sheets of paper. This provides a certain springiness for the nib. Too hard a surface, such as only one or two sheets of paper, will not produce smooth strokes.

BODY MECHANICS

While most strokes can be made with a balanced movement of only the three fingers holding the pen, it is important to take a look at the other parts of the hand and arm. A stroke made by moving only your fingers would make a flat arc, almost a straight line. A stroke made from the wrist yields an arc that is longer and straighter. And the stroke made moving the arm from the elbow gives an even longer arc that is closer to a straight line than the previous two arcs (see figure 17). All parts of

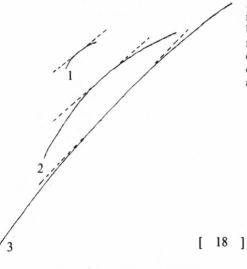

Fig. 17. Body mechanics. 1) Stroke made by fingers only. 2) Stroke made by movement of wrist. 3) Stroke made by movement of arm from the elbow. Dotted line in each stroke indicates part of arc that approximates a straight line.

the body describe arcs in their movement from the joints. To make straight lines—for some strokes—all that will be necessary will be the short finger movements. Others will require movement from the wrist and still others, from the elbow. As we discuss the 45° angle exercise (on page 30) and other strokes, you will see how this can be useful.

HOW TO HOLD THE PEN

Place the pen between your thumb and slightly bent forefinger, resting it on your middle finger, and in the crook of your hand and in line with your arm (see figures 18, 19, and 20). You are thus setting up a tripodal arrangement between these three fingers to obtain the best equilibrium possible. The forefinger offsets pressure from the thumb, the thumb counterbalances pressure from the forefinger, and the middle finger prevents too much lateral pressure. This creates even, balanced pressure across the surface of the nib.

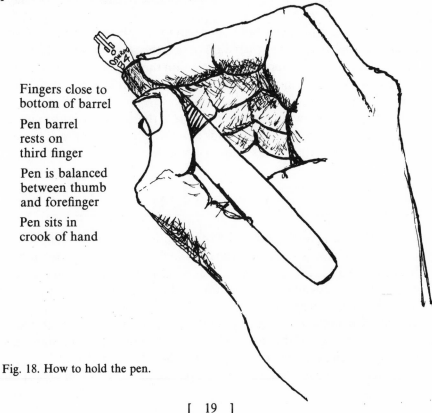

Fingers close to bottom of barrel

Pen barrel rests on third finger

Pen is balanced between thumb and forefinger

Pen sits in crook of hand

Fig. 18. How to hold the pen.

[19]

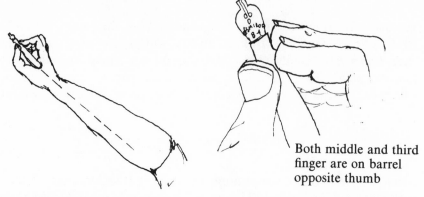

Both middle and third
finger are on barrel
opposite thumb

Fig. 19. The pen in line with the arm.   Fig. 20. One way *not* to hold the pen.

Do not hold the pen too tightly between thumb and forefinger. This will eventually cause your fingers to cramp. Do not apply too much pressure on the middle finger, as this will cause development of a callous that may eventually become painful. On the other hand, holding the pen too loosely will not give you sufficient control over movement of the pen.

The angle at which you hold your pen to the plane of the paper also has some importance. Try to avoid holding the pen too vertically to the paper. This will cause too much friction on the nib, and could bend the nib when the pen is moved. Instead, hold the pen at a relatively shallow angle to the plane of the paper.

When you write with your fountain pen, there is no need to put the cap on the back end. This only adds dead weight to your pen; your objective is to have the pen as light as possible.

PEN PRESSURE

Even pressure across the surface of the nib is important. Too much pressure on one side of the nib edge or the other can damage the nib by bending one of the three prongs, sometimes irreparably. Even pressure will produce a stroke of full width of the nib; uneven pressure will often produce a stroke with ragged sides. Avoid pressing too hard with your thumb on the left edge of the nib, or too hard with your forefinger on the right edge of the nib. Neither finger should be dominant (see figure 21). (The fingers are reversed for the left-handed.)

To help you insure balanced pressure, hold a ruler as you would the

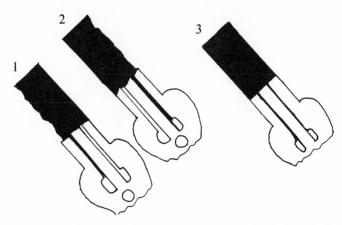

Fig. 21. Uneven nib pressure. 1) Too much pressure on right edge, too little on left edge. 2) Too much pressure on left edge, too little on right edge. 3) Even lateral pressure.

pen, and write using the ruler. Seeing yourself writing on such a large scale (without ink) may help you diagnose whether you are applying uneven pressure.

PLAYING WITH THE PEN

To get used to the feel of your pen, try playing a little with it, moving it in different directions (see figure 22). Remember to always apply even pressure across the surface of the nib in any direction you move the pen.

Fig. 22. Playing with the pen. Get used to the feel of the pen, proper balance, and even pressure on the nib.

NOTES FOR THE LEFT-HANDED

Sit at the table in the same way as I suggest for right-handed writers; that is, feet flat on floor, chair close to writing table, relaxed, and facing straight.

If you write normally holding a pen upside down, you may find it

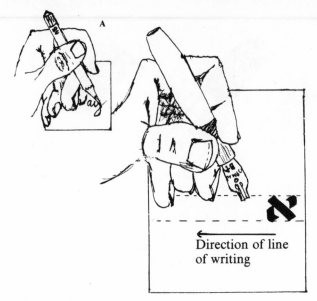

Direction of line
of writing

Fig. 23. How to hold the pen for the left–handed. If you normally hold a pen as in (a), hold the broad–nibbed pen the same way.

easier to do calligraphy in the same way (see figure 23). In such a case the paper will be placed centered in front of you (see page 18 for centering.)

If you write normally with your paper slanted, and a pen at right angles to your hand, then there are two possible ways to place the paper and hold the pen: either slant the paper (sometimes making it almost parallel to your body), hold the pen across your hand, and write away from you, or else hold the paper vertically and write almost upside down (see figure 24).

HOLDING THE PEN
Depending upon how you normally hold a pen when writing, figure 24 will show you how to hold the pen and paper.

A NOTE FOR THE LEFT-HANDED
If you are left-handed, you have been living in a world where you have had to adjust to many things. You have had to learn how to write a different way (sometimes forced into unnatural positions by teachers), to deal with right-handed tools, doors, handles, can-openers, scissors, etc. You have probably developed an innovative approach to living in a right-handed world. But you are in good company: Leonardo Da Vinci and Michelangelo, to name two, were left-handed.

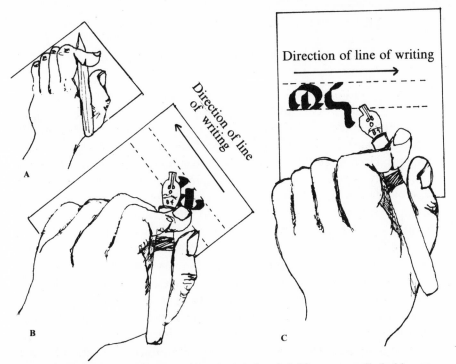

Fig. 24. Other ways to hold the pen for the left–handed. If you normally hold a pen as in (a), hold the broad–nibbed pen as in (b) (with the paper slanted) or as in (c) (with the paper upside down).

As you begin to practice calligraphy, a few things may be awkward at first, such as the way you have to hold the pen to insure a correct angle or the slant of the paper or the direction in which you will be writing. But it is worth the effort.

Both Osmiroid and Platignum pens make nibs for use by left–handed writers. They are called "oblique," or "left–handed," nibs (see figure 25). The edge of the nib is slanted so that it is easier for left–handed writers to maintain the necessary angles (see figure 26).

Fig. 25. Oblique B–4 nib. The slanted edge makes it easier for left–handed writers to maintain pen angles.

Fig. 26. Straight B–4 nib (a) compared with oblique (left–handed) B–4 nib (b). While edges of both nibs are at the same angle, the pens are not parallel to each other.

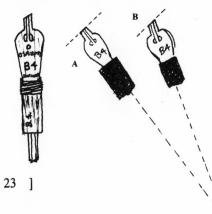

[23]

RELAXATION BEFORE WRITING

Before beginning to work, sit down, relax, and close your eyes. Sit with both feet on the floor, hands in front of you, back straight but not rigid. Relax the shoulders and back of the neck. Take a slow deep breath through your nose, breathing in deeply from the chest down to the diaphragm. Hold it, and then breathe out from diaphragm to chest, slowly and evenly. Then pause before taking in another breath. The process should begin with a slow short count, like "one . . . two . . . three . . .," taking that long to breathe in; then hold; then count a slow three as you breathe out. Repeat the process, increasing the count by one for each cycle, until you are able to count slowly to six or seven for each breath. While you are doing this breathing, try to relax your shoulders, back of the neck, forehead, forearm, hands, and fingers. I find that these parts of the body get most tense during work. The breathing exercise also slows down your pulse just a little. It's important not to rush in any of your work but to go as slowly as possible. This gives you more control over your strokes, and enables you to give more concentration to each stroke.

3

Theory and Practice

STROKE ELEMENTS

Each stroke made by the pen consists of four discrete, yet coherent and connected, elements. One element leads to the next until the stroke is completed. But each must be understood to make the stroke correctly.

The four elements are:

1. *Placement of the Pen.* It is important to place the nib at the exact spot where the stroke begins. Careful and precise placement of the nib insures sharp, disciplined, and straight letters. After the nib has been placed, you are ready to move.

2. *Movement.* Apply pressure to the nib (which will create friction to draw ink out of the pen) and move the pen smoothly, slowly, applying even pressure to both sides of the nib, and consistently in the direction that the stroke is made.

3. *Stopping Movement.* The middle finger acts as a brake to stop the pressure of the thumb and forefinger. Release completely the pressure on the nib at the end of the stroke.

4. *Lifting of the Pen.* Lift the pen straight up from the paper. It is

important that the pressure be completely released from the nib *before* the pen is lifted. This provides sharply defined letters.

Though each step is separate, they are to be done in fluid sequence. It is often the tendency of beginning students to stop writing and lift the pen in one motion. Be sure that you have completely stopped movement and completely released pressure on the nib *before* you lift the pen.

PROPORTION AND INTRINSIC CHARACTERISTICS

Letters have internal proportion, and proportions exist between letters. The internal proportions give beauty to each letter; the proportions between letters give beauty to an alphabet or script as a whole. Other aspects—such as spacing and layout—also contribute to the beauty of calligraphy.

How do letters look proportional? Or: What makes a letter a letter? To begin with, they have what I call their *intrinsic characteristics.* Each letter maintains a certain quality that lets the viewer know that he is seeing a certain letter. This intrinsic characteristic makes each letter unique and independent; if it is significantly distorted, the letter ceases to be recognizable. (Intrinsic characteristics will be pointed out in the textual part of the plates.)

Let us look at the letters *yod* י and *vav* ו. If I take a *yod* and extend its vertical stroke, it becomes a *vav.* If I extend the horizontal stroke of the *yod,* it is not easily recognizable as a *yod* . If I extend vertical and horizontal strokes equally, the *yod* turns into a *resh* ר. The relationship of the parts of a letter to each other determines what that letter is. This proportional relationship is one of the qualities that determines intrinsic characteristic. (Letters in the plates have been grouped together by similar intrinsic characteristics.)

NIB-UNITS

How does one determine the size of letters as well as the proper proportions between elements of a letter? With the aid of a standard of measurement known as the nib-unit.

A nib-unit is equal to the width of the nib you are using; it is the

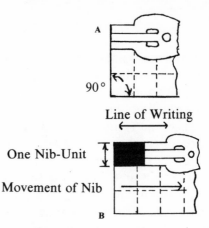

90°

Line of Writing
⟵⟶

Fig. 27. One nib–unit. a) Placement
of nib at 90° angle to line of writing
prior to movement. b) Movement of
nib in line of writing to form nib–unit
stroke.

One Nib-Unit

Movement of Nib

B

widest stroke you can make with your pen. As such, it is a relative unit
of measurement determined by the pen with which you are writing.
For the basic script (taught in the plates), I am using a system whereby
three nib-units determine the height of a letter such as an *alef* or a *resh*.

But before you can make three nib-units, you need to know how to
make *one* nib-unit. To make a nib-unit, you must know in which direction you are writing. I call this the line of writing (shown in figure
27). Now hold your pen so that the edge of the nib is perpendicular—
that is, at exactly 90°—to the line of writing (A), and then move the nib
in the direction of the line of writing (B).

In making nib-units, since the edge of the nib is perpendicular to the
line of writing, it is also perpendicular to your body, and since your
pen is held in line with your arm, this means that your arm will be
parallel to the edge of the table (as in figure 28A). Movement of the
entire arm is not necessary. You need only bring thumb and forefinger
simultaneously in toward your palm, with a balanced and even movement.

If you are left-handed, the paper will be held parallel to you, so that
the line of writing is perpendicular to you. Then you will be pulling the
stroke toward you (see figure 28B).

Fig. 28. Position of arms for making nib–units. a) Right–handed. b) Left–handed.

A

B

If the nib is not exactly perpendicular to the line of writing, the nib-unit width will not be at its widest; similarly, if the pen is not exactly in line with the line of writing, the direction in which the nib-unit is drawn will not be correct.

Once you've made one nib-unit, it's a pretty simple task to make three. Begin the second nib-unit by placing the right edge of the nib at the lower right-hand corner of the previous nib-unit, and then make another nib-unit. Make the third nib-unit like the second (see figure 29). The purpose of drawing nib-units in this stepwise pattern is to know exactly where one ends and the next one begins. If each nib-unit were to be placed directly alongside the previous one, you wouldn't see where one ended and the next one began, and so would not be able to mark off an exact measurement of three nib-units.

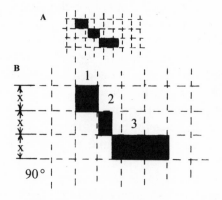

Fig. 29. Three nib–units. a) Three nib–units as made by a B–4 nib (actual size), with dotted lines to indicate graph paper lines (ten squares per inch). b) Enlargement of (a). Note how the width—"X"—of each nib–unit is the same, while the length of the nib–unit may vary, as in (1), (2), and (3), depending upon how long the stroke is made. Notice also how the step arrangement—each nib–unit touches only the corner of the previous one—allows you to see where each nib–unit begins and ends, and gives an exact view of three nib–units.

Three nib-units is the determination for the height of a letter such as *vet* or *mem.* So a pen ¼″ wide will produce a letter in the basic script such as *vet* or *mem,* one that is ¾″ high, or three nib-units of that particular pen.

This height is the height of the main body line. But in Hebrew (as in other languages) some letters descend or ascend above the main body line. Examples of descenders would be final *fe*, final *nun*, or any letter that extends below the main body line. In Hebrew there is only one ascender, the *lamed*. In the case of the basic script you'll be learning, the central line will be three nib-units high, and descenders will extend two nib-units below the line, while the ascender (the *lamed*) will extend two nib-units above the line. In terms of spacing, this means that a minimum of four nib-units between main body lines must be maintained in order to accommodate both an ascender from one line and a descender from a previous line. (See page 41 for a full discussion of spacing.) With a few exceptions, such as *ayin* and *fe*, all letters will follow this system.

It should be noted that these proportions of three nib-units for basic letter height do not hold for every script. For examples of other proportional nib-unit relations, see pages 91–93, following the basic script.

ANGLES

Only when the nib is held at a 90° angle (perpendicular) to the line of writing will the stroke made by the pen be the widest possible. And the stroke—if the pen is pulled in a straight line, and exactly in line with the line of writing—will be a rectangle. If, however, the pen nib is held at any other angle to the line of writing than 90°, the stroke will be less wide and will be in the shape of a parallelogram. (See figure 30.) Notice also that the width of the stroke is determined by the angle at which the nib is held in relation to the line of writing, but the length of

Fig. 30. Strokes made by holding the nib at different angles. Any other nib angle will produce a stroke of lesser width. 1) Only holding the pen at a 90° angle to the line of writing will give the widest stroke possible for any given nib. 2) This is the stroke produced with the nib at a 45° angle (indicated by the dot–dash line). This stroke is approximately two-thirds as wide as a nib–unit. 3) This is the stroke produced with the nib at 0° to the line of writing (i.e., *in line* with the line of writing).

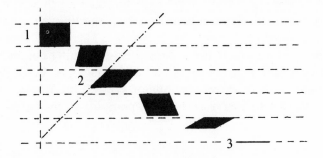

the stroke can be long or short, depending upon how long the pen is pulled in the direction of the line of writing.

In the basic script, the nib will be held at a 90° angle only when making nib-units. You will also notice that if the paper you are using is graph paper with ten squares per inch, and the nib is a B-4, then the stroke made when holding the nib at a 90° angle will be exactly as wide as the distance between two lines on the graph paper. In this way the paper will help to guide you in practicing nib-units and in determining letter proportions.

Though the nib is held only at a 90° angle when making nib-units, it is still extremely important to know how to hold your nib at a 90° angle. You won't always have exactly proportioned graph paper, and you will need to know how to determine the proportions for any script. Finally, there are scripts in which a 90° angle is used to form the letters. (See page 92 for an example of such a script.)

THE 45° ANGLE

While 90° is the angle at which to hold the nib for making nib-units, the 45° angle is the one that is most important for forming the letters in the basic script. A 45° angle is exactly half of a 90° angle. (See figure 30.) Holding the pen at a 45° angle will bisect a square; that is, it will divide a square in half along a diagonal, forming two triangles.

Since the angle of the nib to the line of writing is 45°, and since you hold the pen in line with the arm, this means that your arm will be held at a 45° angle to the edge of the table.

To train your hand and eye to hold the pen at a 45° angle, there is a good exercise you can practice (see figure 31). In this exercise, often called "hills and valleys," the pen is held so that the nib is at a 45° angle, and the pen is moved at a 45° angle for both up and down strokes.

Before beginning the 45° angle exercise, take a pencil and straight edge and draw a horizontal line on one of the lines of graph paper. Make three nib-units hanging from this line. Then draw another horizontal pencil line at the bottom of the third nib-unit. (You may simply count three graph paper boxes if you wish, since you know that these are the equivalent of three nib-units of a B-4 nib.) This is the three-nib-unit line that will serve as the focal point for all the letters you will

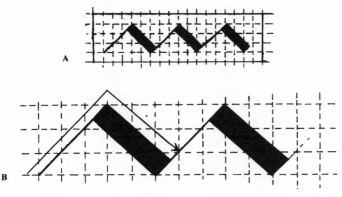

Fig. 31. 45° angle excercise (the "hills and valleys"). a) Done actual size with a B–4 nib. b) An enlargement of (a). Note how the lines going up are the thinnest possible, while lines going down are thickest possible.

be doing. A *khaf* כ or *mem* מ or *shin* ש would be placed on this three-nib-unit line, while a final *fe* ף or a *kof* ק would descend two nib-units below this three-nib-unit line, and a *lámed* ל would ascend two nib-units above this three-nib-unit line.

From now on, I will refer to this line when I discuss placement of the nib for each stroke in a letter. Reference will generally be made to the top or bottom of the three-nib-unit line.

It's important to always draw these horizontal lines. These are your guidelines for the three-nib-unit line, and for your letters. The top and bottom line provide you with a visual frame for making your strokes.

With the three-nib-unit line drawn, begin the 45° angle exercise by placing the nib in the corner of a box on your graph paper at the bottom of the three-nib-unit line. Place the left edge of the nib in the corner at a 45° angle. This means that you are aiming the right edge of the nib to the opposite corner of the box.

(Throughout the execution of any stroke, always be aware of the right and left edges of the nib. In making strokes, either the right or left edge of the nib will be used as a guide, or leading edge.)

With the left edge of the nib placed in the corner of a box at the bottom of the three-nib-unit line, and the nib at a 45° angle, aim the right edge of the nib through the upper right-hand corner of the box. Move the nib through three boxes—exactly from corner to corner of each box—until the right edge of the nib reaches the top of the three-nib-unit line. Pause before making the downward part of the exercise. Then bring the pen downward, using the left edge of the nib as a guide and bringing this edge through the corners of the boxes as the nib is brought downward. Pulling the left edge of the nib through the corners of three boxes brings the nib to the bottom of the three-nib-unit line, so that its left edge ends up once more in the corner of a box in preparation for the upward part of the exercise. This means that it is never necessary to lift the nib off the paper; it is only necessary to pause (to change direction) at the end of each upward and downward movement. Repeat the exercise. (See figures 31 and 32A.)

There are a number of important points to note in this 45° angle exercise:

- It should never be necessary to lift the pen from the paper during several cycles of the "hills and valleys." Only when you run out of paper should you have to lift the pen.
- If the nib is held at a 45° angle, and the pen is moved at a 45° angle upward, the thinnest line possible is made. Conversely, moving the pen downward at a 45° angle while maintaining a nib angle of 45° will produce the widest stroke possible.
- When moving the pen upward, the right edge of the nib becomes the leading edge and guide for the stroke, and the thumb becomes the propelling part of the arm—that is, the thumb leads the rest of the arm in moving the pen upward on the edge of the nib and at a 45° angle. The rest of the arm merely follows.
- The movement of the arm in the upward part of the exercise describes an arc, but the length of the arc is long and flat, and approximates a straight line. Avoid moving only your thumb and forefinger. Movement of the hand from the wrist might describe an arc sufficiently flat to describe a consistently thin straight line for the short distance needed (three graph boxes), but movement from the elbow *guarantees* such a consistently thin straight line.
- When moving the pen downward for the wide stroke (the "downhill"), the arm mechanics are different. Movement of the pen is the same as that in making a nib-unit. Thus, only the thumb and forefinger are used. They are now brought simultaneously closer to the hand in balance with each other, neither one being dominant over the other. Even pressure across the entire edge of the nib is important, and should be insured by balance between thumb and forefinger.
- When normally holding the pen, the fingers are at a certain optimum distance from the palm. At the completion of the downward stroke of the 45° angle exercise, the fingers have been brought into

the hand, reducing this distance. Before beginning the next upward stroke, it is necessary to regain this distance. Do this by *moving the heel of your hand away from the pen* while the fingers remain stationary so that the nib is still in contact with the paper. Then you are ready to resume the exercise. Before doing so, however, move the paper—with the nib still on the paper—so that the nib is at your "center" spot. If the distance of the fingers from the palm is not readjusted, or the pen (and paper) not returned to center, you will not be able to maintain a nib angle of 45 ° as you continue the exercise. Always maintain this angle, in this exercise and throughout the coming plates.

- You are succeeding in this exercise when a line of "hills and valleys" looks consistent.

This exercise is not only a good one for training you to maintain a nib angle of 45 °, but it's also a useful warm-up exercise to do each time you sit down to practice your letters.

It is important to notice what happens when the 45 ° angle exercise is done incorrectly. This can be seen in figure 32D. These errors result from incorrect nib angle or incorrect direction of movement, or a combination of both.

PRELIMINARY EXERCISES

Once you've worked on maintaining a 45 ° nib angle, there are other practice strokes that can be helpful before you move on to the first letter (see figure 32E, F).

First, here is an exercise in making vertical strokes. Place the right edge of the nib at the top of the three-nib-unit line, and the left edge of the nib touching a vertical graph line. (If you are left-handed, you may find it easier—though not necessarily so—to place the right edge of your nib at the top of the three-nib-unit line *and* in the upper right-hand corner of a graph box.) Check your nib angle. When the nib is placed at a 45 ° angle, the distance from the upper left-hand corner of the graph box will be the same from both the left and right edges of the nib. Bring the nib down to the bottom of the three-nib-unit line, using the left edge of the nib as a guide. End the stroke when the left edge of the nib reaches the bottom of the three-nib-unit line.

For the next exercise, place the nib at the same starting point, but

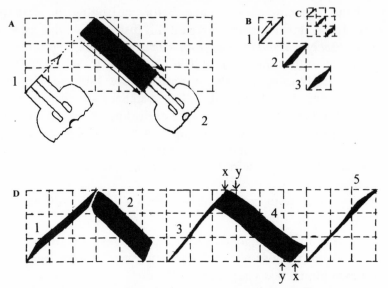

Fig. 32. More on the 45° angle. a) The 45° angle exercise, shown to emphasize that on the up stroke (1) aim the nib, on its edge, through the corners of each square, using the thumb as the leading guide for movement. On the down stroke (2) both thumb and forefinger are brought into the hand, in a balanced movement. The downward stroke is equal to a nib–unit in width. b) The quick test for a 45° angle. Place the nib precisely in the corner of a square. Move the nib a very short distance, aiming exactly to the opposite corner. (1) is the result of a 45° angle—i.e., the thinnest line possible. (2) and (3) are results of incorrect angle—a diamond–shaped stroke results. c) The quick test (as in (b)), shown actual size, using a B–4 nib. d) The 45° angle exercise done incorrectly. (1) is the nib at an incorrect angle, but moved correctly through the corners of each square. (2) is the down stroke of (1) and not as wide as the correctly done stroke (as in (a)). (3) is the nib not moved precisely through the corners of each square, arriving at "x" when it should have arrived at "y." While (3) and (4) might appear as the correct exercise, movement of the nib was not precise. (5) is the up stroke done where the nib angle changed as the nib arrived near the last corner. e) Vertical and horizontal practice strokes made with the nib at a 45° angle. Note that horizontal and vertical strokes will be the same width (x) if the nib is held at the correct angle. In (1), the left edge of the nib is placed on a vertical graph line, with the right edge of nib at the top of the three–nib–unit line. Move the pen downward, using the left edge of the nib as guide, until the left edge reaches the bottom of the three–nib–unit line. In (2), place the right edge of the nib at the top of the three–nib–unit line, with the left edge on the vertical graph line. Move the pen to the right, using the right edge of the nib as guide. In (3), a horizontal stroke is made as in (2), but along the bottom of the three–nib–unit line, with the left edge of the nib as guide. f) Horizontal and vertical practice strokes shown actual size as made with a B–4 nib. g) Vertical and horizontal strokes done with the nib at incorrect angles. Even though (1) and (4) are of equal width, and (2) and (3) are of equal width, (1) and (3) are the two strokes made with the same (incorrect) nib angle, and (2) and (4) are also two strokes made with the same (incorrect) nib angle.

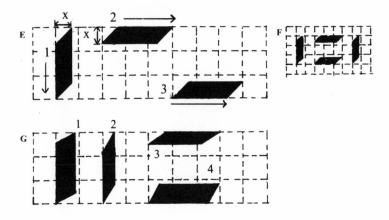

make a horizontal stroke. Use the right edge of the nib as a guide along the top of the three-nib-unit line. Make another horizontal stroke using the left edge of the nib as a guide along the bottom of the three-nib-unit line. Begin the stroke by placing the left edge of the nib at the bottom of the three-nib-unit line.

If the nib is correctly maintained at a 45° angle in these exercises, both horizontal strokes and vertical strokes should be of equal width (see figure 32E). If you find they are not of equal width (as in figure 32G), the nib is not at a 45° angle.

Note also that neither horizontal strokes nor vertical strokes will ever be as wide as a nib-unit. Holding the nib at a 45° angle will always produce a stroke that is a parallelogram, approximately two-thirds as wide as the nib-unit stroke.

Finally, there is a quick test for the nib angle of 45° (see figure 32B, C). Place the left edge of the nib in any lower left-hand corner of any graph box. Aim the right edge of the nib toward the upper right-hand corner of that box. Move the nib toward the corner. Stop when the right corner of the nib reaches the upper right-hand corner of the box. Lift the pen. If the stroke you have made is the thinnest possible, the nib is at a 45° angle. Anything other than the thinnest line possible—a diamond-shaped stroke, for example—means that you must rotate the pen slightly to find the 45° angle.

II
THE PLATES

Introduction
to the Plates

As you work from one section to the next, the elements you will have learned combine to form new letters. Each time you learn a new letter, keep in mind that this letter is based on previous structural elements, and the discipline involved in forming the strokes of previous letters. Never assume you "know" the elements so well that you can rush through a new letter. For the letters to be beautiful, each individual element must be understood and formed carefully. Give your attention to each element at the moment you are making it, and everything you have learned so far will come together in that moment as you write. Whenever you form any element as part of a letter, you must concentrate on that element only. It's a question of staying with the present, and not thinking about the past (the element you just formed a minute ago) or the future (the elements you'll need to make next to complete the letter).

ON PRACTICING

The real foundation of your work is practice. Be patient with yourself and keep practicing until the strokes are perfect. Of course, you have to make sure you're perfecting the right thing! So look carefully at the letter, study it, and practice it.

At the same time, you have to really feel the letter as it's made by your hand, not merely as you see it with your eyes. You have to let the letter get inside you. When you are first learning a letter, it's sometimes helpful to put a piece of tracing paper over the letter and trace it with your pen to get a sense of the strokes and their proportions.

Another, more important way to gain an inner understanding of the letter is to put your pen on the paper at the point you are going to begin the first stroke, and then close your eyes (yes, that's what I said!) and make the letter with your eyes closed. This technique does several things. First of all, it forces you to slow down just at the point when most people are going too fast. Slowing down allows you to *think* about what you are doing, instead of making strokes automatically. You begin to understand the movements necessary to form the letter, and the structural elements of that letter. It's also an excellent way to concentrate—even to meditate—upon the letter, that is, focus on it to the exclusion of anything else. Finally, the letter gets *inside* you, "into your hand," and you have a clear mental picture of what you are doing. Try it with each letter. You'll be surprised at what occurs when you make a letter with your eyes closed. You might even find that your letters look *better* done that way.

Once you learn a letter, and practice it, don't just move on to the next letter, and then the one after that. Since we are building up letters, and since, in writing out texts, one never writes words of only one letter, it is important to start combining letters as you go along. This enables you to practice previous letters while you learn new ones. It also enables you to learn to move from letter to letter and maintain your disciplined approach to letters as you make words. Finally, letter combinations are more interesting than isolated letters!

This kind of practice is very valuable. After you have learned a number of new letters well, you can begin work on spacing of letters and spacing of words. Use combinations of letters as you learn them to make up your own words. These words don't have to mean anything; the important thing is to learn to move easily from letter to letter while making words. An example of a first word might be something like

וו״ר

(*yavan,* Greece). Other beginning words might be

(*rooaḥ,* wind or spirit) or

(*haf,* which means nothing; it is simply a combination of two letters you'll learn early on). Following each letter group in the plates will be a list of suggested words to use for practicing combinations of letters.

SPACING

Part of the balanced, pleasing look of fine calligraphy comes from a sense of consistent spacing. In writing out words, you'll want to make sure that both the spaces between letters and the spaces between words are consistent (see figure 33). (Don't begin to worry about spacing,

Fig. 33. Spacing.

however, until you are well into the plates. There's no need to divide your concentration until you have achieved familiarity and a degree of proficiency with the letters.) Try to get your letters close to each other (but not touching). Experiment a little with varying the spaces between letters, and see what happens. You might combine a *lamed* and a *vet* and tuck the right extension of the *vet* under the canopy of the *lamed:*

Or you might put a *yod* and *gimmel* together:

Try also to maintain the same distance between words each time you write. This space should be the width of an *alef,* that is, three nib-units wide. I myself tend to discourage students from thinking of letters in terms of numbers of nib-units wide, as I feel that the mental visualization of a letter is more important. While I do offer a kind of visual crutch by the use of graph paper, eventually you will abandon this crutch by working on unlined paper (where you draw pencil lines only of the top and bottom horizontal lines of the three-nib-unit line), and by learning to write with your eyes closed so you can mentally "see" what the letter actually looks like.

Spacing between lines is determined as follows. Let's begin with the basic three-nib-unit line. To make room for descenders (as in the final forms), two nib-units are required. To make room for the ascender, *lamed,* coming up from the next line, another two nib-units are required. So far, we have a total of four nib-units between the basic three-nib-unit lines. To prevent a descender from touching the *lamed,* let's add another nib-unit. This gives us a five nib-unit space between basic lines, and a spacing of lines that looks like this: three nib-units (a basic line), five nib-units, three nib-units (another basic line), five nib-units, three nib-units, and so on. (When doing a project, which we'll discuss after the plates, you may find it useful to leave more space between basic lines, say ten nib-units.) Take a look at some of the quotations in this book for examples of spacing.

REMINDERS

- Slow down. The slower you go, the faster you'll learn.
- Center yourself.
- Remember the four elements for every stroke.
- Concentrate only on the stroke at hand. Do not anticipate the next stroke, or the next letter.
- Keep checking the 45° nib angle.
- Always go slower on curved strokes.

- Most strokes are made by pulling the pen. Some strokes are made by pushing the pen. For the latter it's important to keep the pen at a shallow angle to the plane of the paper.
- Remember to pay attention to the numbers and arrows accompanying the strokes of the letters.
- Always draw pencil lines at the top and bottom of the three-nib-unit line. When you come to the descenders (and the ascender) draw a pencil line two nib-units below the three-nib-unit line (and two nib-units above the three-nib-unit line for the *lamed*).
- Precise placement of the nib is important. *Just* touch the corner of the nib where it should be, either as a first stroke, or as a second (or third) stroke just touches the first stroke.
- When practicing, it's a good idea to date your practice sheets. In this way you will gain an overview of how you are doing from week to week.

NOTES ON THE PLATES

The following plates are grouped according to basic characteristics. There are six groups. The letters in this basic script are presented in the simplest form. Each letter has intrinsic characteristics which define and distinguish that letter from any other letter, and these characteristics will often be pointed out in the text accompanying the plates. New letters are introduced as they combine previously learned strokes and their characteristics. Each group of plates is made up of letters of similar characteristics.

The letters done in large format, and as part of the instruction for each letter, were written with a Soennecken 100A ¼″ wide dip pen. Each letter that occurs in the written text of each plate, right after the name of the letter, is written with a B-4 Osmiroid nib, so that you may see it in the actual size in which you will be working.

A "stroke" is a complete motion of the pen. "Element" means part of a stroke.

A NOTE ON THE FINAL FORMS

If you look at the final forms of letters, you'll notice that in most cases the final form is a simple variation of the regular form. By taking the bottom horizontal stroke of the *khaf,* for example, and rotating it 90° to turn it into a vertical stroke, you achieve the *khaf sofit.* The same can be seen with *nun sofit, fe sofit,* and *tzaddi sofit:*

Mem sofit is a bit anomalous:

מ ם

THE *YOD* GROUP

The letters in this group use *yod* as a basic element in their formation. By extending the *yod* horizontally and/or vertically, different letters can be created. *Yod* is the first letter in God's name, and indeed the *yod* can be seen in almost every letter in the Hebrew alphabet.

[44]

This is the letter yod ◀.   **YOD**
Most of the letters in this
basic script (and subsequent
scripts in this book) use yod
as an essential element in their con·
struction. Begin the yod by placing the
right edge of the pen nib at the top of
the ~~three-nib-unit line~~ (A). Keep the nib at
a 45° angle and pull it in a slow contin-
uous movement made up of three
parts: 1. horizontal; 2. a curve to
change direction; 3. vertical, straight
down. Stop halfway down the three-
nib-unit line.
In these diagrams, arrows indicate
where to begin the stroke and in
what direction it is made. The
stroke ends where the arrow ends.

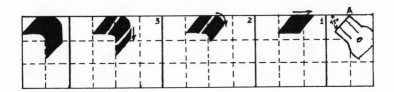

VAV

ו

The letter vav ו is formed in almost the same way as the yod. However, make the horizontal element shorter than that of the yod. In the vav it should be just long enough to express horizontality. Also, extend the vertical element so that the left edge of the nib just touches the bottom line of the three-nib-unit line. The vav's intrinsic characteristics are: It is short in its horizontal element on top (so as not to be confused with the resh); it must not be too short vertically (so as not to be confused with the yod); and it must not extend below the three-nib-unit line (or it may be confused with nun sofit).

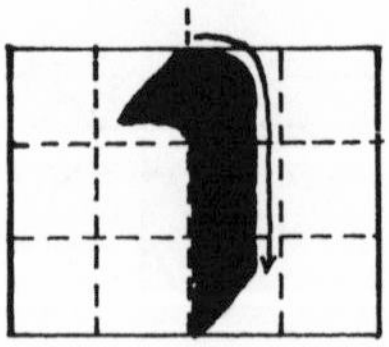

Nun sofit (final nun)
is formed like the vav.
It is very short horizontally,
just long enough to express
horizontality, and this also
enables the nun sofit to con-
form stylistically with the vav.
The only difference in making nun
sofit is that you extend the vertical
element two nib-units <u>below</u> the
three-nib-unit line (that is, until the
left edge of the nib touches a line two
nib-units below the three-nib-unit line).
Because it extends below the three-nib-
unit line, nun sofit is called a descender.

NUN SOFIT

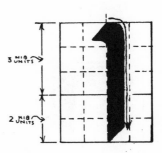

RESH Form resh ⊐ in the same manner as yod but make its horizontal element at least as long as the vertical. Visually, resh appears to have two equal parts—horizontal and vertical—joined by a bend in the upper right-hand corner. The vertical element is as in vav, while the horizontal element is much longer. Do not make the horizontal element too short; its length is the intrinsic characteristic of the resh. (We will see later that resh, and several other letters, may be lengthened horizontally in order to justify a line.)

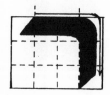

In forming khaf sofit **KHAF SOFIT**
(final khaf) ך, make a
resh, but continue
the vertical element
until it descends two
nib-units below the three-nib-unit
line (as in nun sofit). Like most
final forms, it is a descender.
(Khaf sofit, like resh, may be extended horizontally when necessary to justify a line.) Its intrinsic
characteristics are the horizontal element, which must be equal
in length to that of the resh (so
as not to be confused with nun
sofit), and the vertical element,
which must descend two nib-
units below the
three-nib-unit line (so
as not to be confused
with resh).

HET

Het ת is the first letter made with two strokes. (Number's indicate the order in which the strokes are made.) To form stroke 1, make a resh (with the option of making the horizontal element somewhat shorter). Stroke 2 is vertical. Its placement is important for the balance and beauty of the ḥet. Place the nib so that the left edge is below and in line with the farthest point left of the horizontal element of stroke 1, and the right edge just touches, but doesn't go into, the underside of stroke 1. Bring the nib down, keeping the left edge on a line directly below its starting point.

HE

He ה is formed in the same manner as het, with one significant difference: the second stroke is begun lower than the comparable stroke in the het; it must not have any contact with the first. Begin stroke 2 by placing the nib with its right edge midway down the three-nib-unit line. The left edge of the nib (and the left side of the stroke) is in line with the extreme left point of the horizontal element of stroke 1. The space between strokes 1 and 2 is the intrinsic characteristic of the he, in contrast to that of that of the het, in which the second stroke <u>is</u> attached to the first. (In both het and he, it's important to be sure the nib is at a 45° angle when beginning the second stroke of each letter.)

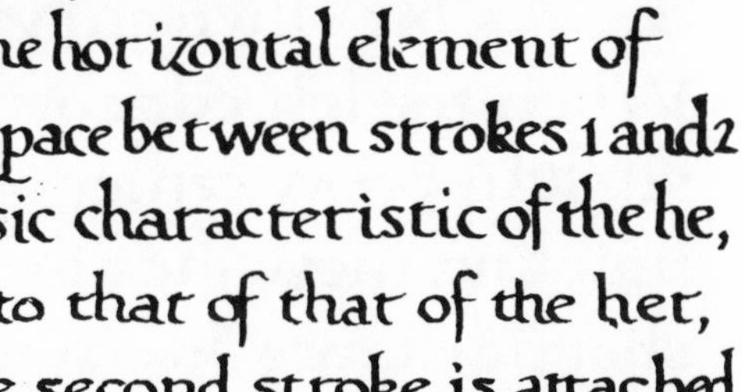

FE SOFIT To begin fe sofit (final fe),
make a khaf sofit. Begin
the second stroke as if you
were making the second
stroke of the het. Place
the left edge of the nib below and
in line with the farthest point left
of the horizontal element of the first
stroke, and just touch the first
stroke with the right edge. Come
down a bit. Then curve to the right.
When the left edge of the nib is
slightly below center of the three-nib-
unit line, move the nib to the right a
short distance. In essence, you have
made an upside-down yod. Do not
make the curve too sharp or too

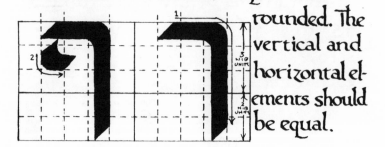

rounded. The
vertical and
horizontal el-
ements should
be equal.

Fe 🔲 is more than
three nib-units high,
which is unusual. Make
a resh, a bit wider than
usual. For the second stroke, align
the left edge of the nib directly below the farthest point left of the
horizontal element of the first stroke.
Then, using the right edge of the nib
as a guide, bring the pen to the
right along the bottom of the three-
nib-unit line until it just touches the
vertical element of the first stroke,
in a perfect join at a 45° angle. This
second stroke is made below the
three-nib-unit line to increase the
visibility of the third stroke which is
formed like the third stroke in fe sofit.

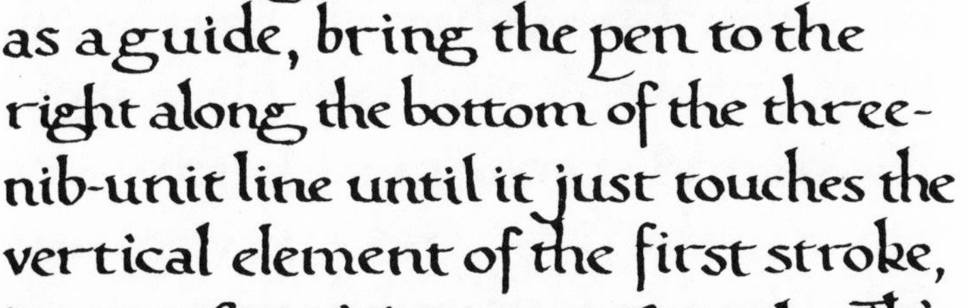

FE

TZADDI SOFIT To form tzaddi sofit (final tzaddi) ץ, first make a nun sofit. Begin the second stroke by placing the right edge of the nib at the top of the three-nib-unit line. Curve the stroke so that it becomes thin as it reaches the center of the three-nib-unit line, where it touches the first stroke. It will look like a <u>shofar</u>. The second stroke must begin very close to the first and curve gracefully and in a balanced manner, not too angular or curved, as it is brought down and to the left.

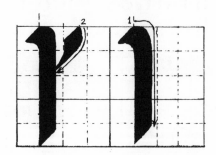

The Yod Group

Words to practice using letters from the *yod* group are:

word	*pronunciation*	*meaning*
יַיִן	yayin	wine
יָוָן	yavan	Greece
רַךְ	rakh	soft
חוֹרֶף	ḥoref	winter
הוֹרָה	horah	hora (a dance)
פַּרְפַּר	parpar	butterfly
פֶּרֶץ	peretz	Peretz (a Yiddish writer)
הַחוֹף	haḥof	the shore
פֶּרַח	peraḥ	flower
הָרֵיחַ	harayaḥ	the scent

THE SLANTED *VAV* GROUP

The letters in this group are all based on the same principle, which I call the slanted *vav*. In essence *gimmel* and *nun* are exactly the same letter, except for the intrinsic characteristics that distinguish the one from the other.

GIMMEL To form gimmel, begin as for vav. Place the right edge of the nib at the top of the three-nib-unit line. Move the pen a short distance on the horizontal. Then curve the stroke and slant the vertical element rightward slightly. This slant must not be too shallow or too deep; the beauty of gimmel depends on balance. Form the second stroke by placing the left edge of the nib on the bottom of the three-nib-unit line, a short distance from the slanted element of stroke 1. (You will learn the correct distance by practice.) Move the pen along the bottom of the three-nib-unit line, using the left edge of the nib as guide, until the right edge touches the first stroke.

like gimmel, nun) is a
balanced letter, but it is
narrower. Begin the first
stroke by placing the right
edge of the nib at the top of the
three-nib-unit line. Make the
shortest possible horizontal
stroke; then curve the stroke and
bring it down on a slant as in the
first stroke of the gimmel. Stop
when the left edge of the nib passes
just below the second nib-unit.
For the second stroke, align the
left edge of the nib with the farthest point left of the beginning
of the first stroke. With the left
edge of the nib as guide, move
the pen along the bottom of the
three-nib-unit line, until the
right edge of the nib
touches the corner
of the first stroke.

NUN

NUN This is an alternate way to make the nun ꓶ -all in one stroke. Begin as in the previous nun, but after the stroke just passes below the second nib-unit, slide the nib on its edge downward to the left at a 45° angle to get the thinnest line possible. Slide until the left edge of the nib touches the bottom of the three-nib-unit line; then push the pen, using the left edge of the nib as guide, until it reaches the point in line with the farthest point left of the top horizontal element. Be careful when pushing the pen not to hold it at too high an angle to the paper or to apply too much pressure. Otherwise you will encounter resistance, which may damage your nib.

TAV

To form the tav רנ, first make a resh. Begin the second stroke as if you were beginning the second stroke of the het, but instead of going straight down, slant the stroke backward and make a one-stroke nun. Be careful not to bring the slanted line too far back or too far below the second nib-unit, so that the slide is as clear as possible. All three left points of the tav should be aligned.

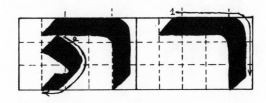

Words to practice using letters from the slanted *vav* group (and the *yod* group) are:

word	pronunciation	meaning
גנת	ginat	garden of
תורה	torah	Torah
נח	noaḥ	Noah
גר	ger	stranger
תוף	tof	drum
חגיגה	ḥagigah	celebration
גרות	nayrot	candles
פנינה	peninah	pearl
תרוץ	tayrootz	solution

THE SQUARED-OFF LETTER, OR WEDGE, GROUP

This group is called the squared-off letter or wedge group because each letter in it is characterized by the same two strokes that meet at the upper right-hand corner of the letter. Note that the plate showing the entire alphabet of this basic script together on one page will sometimes indicate two options for some of the letters: a rounded variant and a squared-off variant. Which variant you decide to use when working on a manuscript is a matter of taste. (Both forms fit within this particular script.) However, be consistent. If you choose the rounded-off variant, stay with it throughout the entire manuscript.

The important thing is that both the rounded-off and squared-off forms must be learned with the same amount of discipline, because each of the two variants give certain letters their intrinsic characteristics. If you look at the *dalet,* you will notice that the only way a *dalet* can be made is with a squared-off corner. And if you look at the *resh,* you'll notice that the only way it can be made is by rounding the upper right-hand corner.

Also look at the *zayin.* It can only be made by making the second stroke so that it begins right from the center of the first stroke, making *zayin* look like a squared-off letter. Placement of this second stroke gives *zayin* the intrinsic characteristic which distinguishes it from a squared-off *vav,* or from a *dalet.*

Only the squared-off *vav,* the *dalet,* and the *zayin* are given complete plates. The other squared-off forms are shown visually only. You need only combine the strokes you learn from *dalet* and the squared-off *vav* to form the squared-off variant.

VAV For the squared-off vav ⸍, place the right edge of the nib at the top of the three-nib-unit line, and move the nib a short distance to the right along the top of the line. For the second stroke, check the pen angle; then place the right edge of the nib just at the lower corner of the first stroke. Now make a vertical stroke that just touches the bottom of the three-nib-unit line. Make sure that the right-hand corner of this squared-off variant is sharp and clear, the two strokes meeting to form one line at a 45° angle.

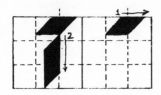

Dalet ７ is formed much like vav. Begin the first stroke as in the vav, but make a stroke approximately three times as long as the horizontal stroke of the vav. For the second stroke, make the second stroke of the vav; with the right edge of the nib just touching the corner of the first stroke, make a vertical stroke. One of the dalet's intrinsic characteristics is that it can be made only as a squared-off letter. Another is that its horizontal stroke must be at least as long as its vertical stroke. This horizontal stroke distinguishes the dalet from the vav.

DALET

ZAYIN

For the zayin 𝗧, make the first stroke approximately one and a half times as long as the first stroke of the squared-off vav, or about half as long as the first stroke of the dalet. (It is useful to observe the relationship of one stroke to another, both within a letter, and in relation to other letters.) For the second stroke, place the right edge of the nib just at the midpoint of the bottom of the first stroke. Now draw the nib back to the right on a slant until its left edge reaches the three-nib-unit line. Placement of the second stroke and the length of the first stroke are intrinsic characteristics that distinguish zayin from vav & dalet.

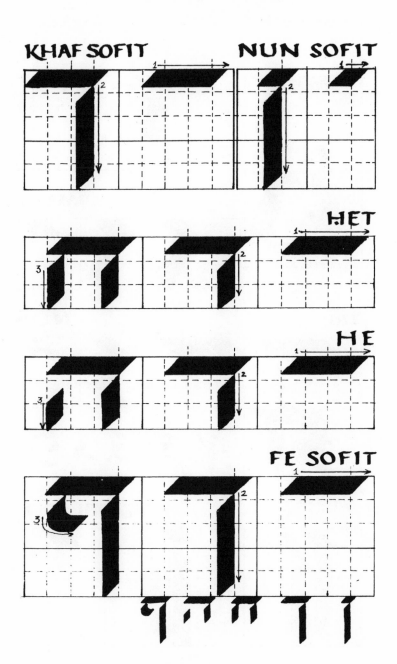

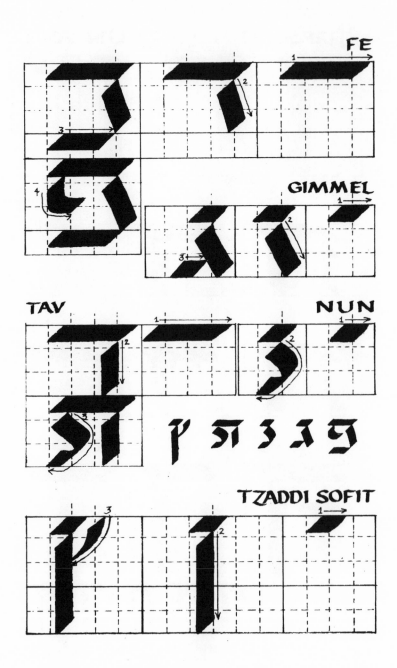

Words to practice using letters from the squared-off group (and previous groups) are:

word	*pronunciation*	*meaning*
זָדוֹן	zadon	wickedness
זַיִן	zayin	the letter *zayin*
דִּינָה	deenah	Dinah
פָּז	paz	fine gold
גְּזֵירָה	g'zayrah	decree

THE TRUNCATED *RESH* GROUP

This group shares one basic characteristic, which I call the truncated *resh*. The vertical stroke of a *resh* is shortened to end just slightly below the second nib-unit, as shown in the following plates.

[69]

KHAF The khaf ⊃ is the model for the truncated resh group. For the first stroke, make a resh. However, end the vertical element when the left edge of the nib reaches just below the second nib-unit. To form the second stroke, place the left edge of the nib at the bottom of the three-nib-unit line, directly below the farthest point left of the horizontal element of the first stroke. Using the left edge of the nib as guide, bring the stroke back until the right edge of the nib meets the corner of the truncated resh stroke. End the stroke at this point.

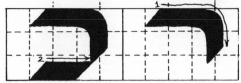

VET

like the khaf, the first stroke of vet ⊐ is a truncated resh that ends slightly below the second nib-unit. Make the second stroke by placing the left edge of the nib on the bottom of the three-nib-unit line and pulling the pen to the right, moving past the end of the first stroke. Remember to align the left points of the two strokes. The intrinsic characteristic of vet, which differentiates it from khaf, is that the second stroke must extend beyond the first.

KOF

To form kof ק, first make a truncated resh. The second stroke is similar to the bottom stroke of the nun. Place the left edge of the nib at the bottom of the three-nib-unit line, a short distance from the first stroke, and move the pen to the right until the right edge of the nib meets the corner of the first stroke. Begin the third stroke as in the second stroke of the het. Make a vertical stroke that ends two nib-units <u>below</u> the three-nib-unit line.

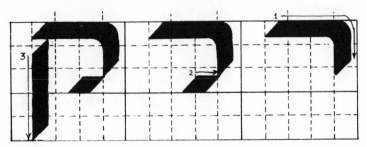

Mem ה is begun
with a vav for the
first stroke. The
second and third

MEM

strokes are the same as the
first and second strokes in kof.
For the second stroke, place the
left edge of the nib just touching the vav. An alternate way
to make mem is to make the
kof strokes first, and then the
vav.

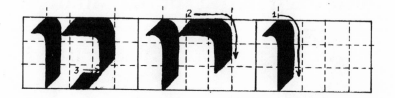

MEM SOFIT

For mem sofit (final mem) D, first make a truncated resh. Begin the second stroke with the second stroke of the het; when you reach the bottom of the three-nib-unit line, pause: stop the motion of the pen, but do not lift the pen from the paper; then continue by making a horizontal line, using the left edge of the nib as a guide along the bottom of the three-nib-unit line, until the right edge of the nib reaches the corner of the truncated resh. The pause in the second stroke produces the square corner in the lower left-hand corner, an in-trinsic characteristic of mem sofit.

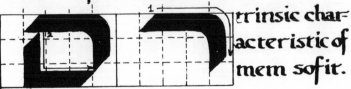

lamed ⌐ is the only let- **LAMED**
ter that ascends
above the basic line.
For the first stroke,
place the right edge of
the nib two nib-units above the
three-nib-unit line and make a
rounded vav. Just as the vav
reaches the top of the three-
nib-unit line, begin to curve
the stroke back, like the last
stroke in the fe (that is, an upside-down yod) and then continue to make a truncated resh.
The second stroke is made in the
same way as that of the kof, taking care that the stroke be short

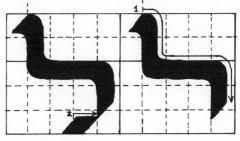

AYIN

Ayin ע is not part of the truncated resh group, but bears similarity to those letters. For the first stroke, make a yod. Begin the second stroke with the nib bisected by the bottom line of the three-nib-unit line, and placed a relatively wide distance away from the first stroke. Then move the nib in a straight line toward the corner of the yod. As the right edge reaches the corner, slide the nib on its edge to line it up with the yod. End the stroke where the yod ends. For the third stroke, place the left edge of the nib directly above the farthest point left of stroke 2 & make a slanted vav.

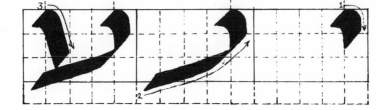

Words to practice using letters from the truncated *resh* group (and previous groups) are:

word	*pronunciation*	*meaning*
כוכב	kokhav	star
בקבוק	bakbook	bottle
מים	mayim	water
עולם	olam	world
גדול	gadol	big
תרנגול	tarn'gol	rooster
מזל	mazal	luck
עדים	aydim	witnesses
זכריה	z'kharyah	Zechariah

word	pronunciation	meaning
מוֹקוּם	makom	place
הַכֹּל	hakol	all
לִפְנֵי	lifnay	before
עוֹף	oaf	fowl
קִבּוּץ	kibbutz	kibbutz

THE ROUNDED LETTER GROUP

The three letters in this group contain the same rounded bottom.

TET

The first stroke of the tet ⟨⟩ is the same as the first stroke of the squared-off vav. The second stroke begins, as in the vav, with the right edge of the nib just touching the corner of the previous stroke. Bring the nib back down to the right in a gentle curve until the left edge reaches the bottom of the three-nib-unit line. Now sharpen the curve slightly, moving up toward the right until the line – now made by the edge of the nib – is at its thinnest. End the stroke at this point. For the third stroke, make a yod that just touches the second stroke.

The shin is formed
in the same way as
the tet, with one addi-
tional stroke. This
fourth stroke is simply a yod
placed in the middle of the tet
so that it comes down straight
to the center.

SHIN

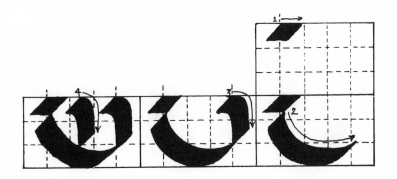

SAMEKH To form samekh ⬤, first make a truncated resh. The second stroke begins in the same manner as the second stroke of the tet, and then curves immediately (though gently and slowly) to the right until it touches the corner of the truncated resh.

Words to practice using letters from the rounded group (and previous groups) are:

word	pronunciation	meaning
שמעון	shimon	Simeon
סופית	sofit	final
טוב	tov	good
טעם	tam	taste
מטבע	matbayah	coin
חטה	ḥeetah	wheat
שלום	shalom	peace
סנהדרין	sanhedrin	Sanhedrin
שטיות	shtooyot	nonsense

[83]

THE ANOMALOUS LETTER GROUP

Alef and *tzaddi* are anomalous because of their diagonal stroke.

ALEF

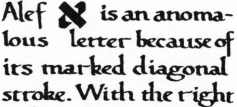

Alef is an anomalous letter because of its marked diagonal stroke. With the right edge of the nib at the top of the three-nib-unit line, make a diagonal stroke three nib-units wide. The second stroke is a yod that comes down with the right edge of the nib aligned with the farthest point right of the diagonal line. End the stroke when it just touches that diagonal. Begin the third stroke with the right edge of the nib just touching the diagonal stroke, and with the left edge in line with the farthest point left of the diagonal stroke. Make an upside-down yod as in the fe.

Begin the tzaddi 𝕫 **TZADDI**
by making the first
stroke of the squared-
off vav. The second
stroke begins at the corner of the
first, then continues to the
right on a very slight diagonal
until it reaches the second nib-
unit of the three-nib-unit line.
Slide the edge of the nib, almost
describing a curve, until the left
edge reaches the bottom of the
three-nib-unit line; then push the
nib to the left until the left edge is
aligned with the farthest point
left of stroke 1. For the third stroke,
place the nib so that it is bisected
by the top three-nib-unit line and
curve it into the second stroke.

Words to practice using letters from the anomalous group (and all previous groups) are:

word	*pronunciation*	*meaning*
אֶרֶץ	aretz	land
יִשְׂרָאֵל	yisrael	Israel
צַדִּיק	tzaddik	a righteous person
צָפוֹן	tzafon	north
אִמָּא	eema	mother
אַבָּא	abba	father
מִצְרַיִם	mitzrayim	Egypt
צִמְחוֹנִי	tzimḥoni	vegetarian

ADDITIONAL PLATES

The next pages contain four plates. The first plate is made up of all the letters in the basic script you have just learned, all on one page. The following three plates show examples of additional scripts. (For additional scripts, see the books by Reuben Leaf and L. F. Toby, listed in the bibliography.) The first part of each plate is the alphabet in the order in which it occurs. The second part is the order in which you should learn the letters for each script. Letters that can be used in justifying a line are denoted by an asterisk (*); those that should be used for justification only when no other letters are available are denoted by a double asterisk (**). As in the plates for the basic script, arrows indicate where to begin each stroke and in what direction it is made. The stroke ends where the arrow ends. Numbers indicate the order in which the strokes are made.

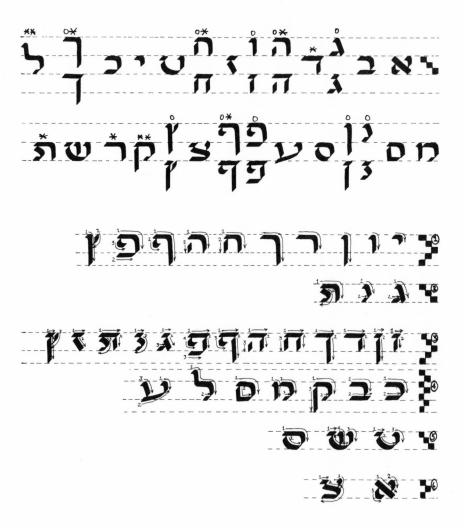

The Basic Script. 1) The *yod* group. 2) The slanted *vav* group. 3) The squared-off letter group. 4) The truncated *resh* group. 5) The rounded letter group. 6) The anomalous letter group. °This symbol indicates when two options—rounded or squared-off—are possible for a letter.

אבגדהוזחטי

כדלמסנסע

פפצקקרשת

ייוודדהחתרם

נתכבופֶפקל

ץקצעשטסגא

Yerushalmi script. This script, called ירושלמי [*Yerushalmi*, Jerusalemite] is based on the lettering used in the Dead Sea Scrolls. The basic line height is five nib-units, with three nib-units for descenders and for the ascender, *lamed.* The nib is held at a 45° angle for all strokes. Almost all letters have a top serif; I have indicated this serif by preliminary strokes A or B. A is used when the stroke following the serif is vertical; B is used when the stroke following the serif is horizontal. In some letters, the serif is made simply by matching the corners of the vertical and horizontal strokes. Many letters also have bottom extensions. These can be extended even more when a decorative effect is desired.

Stam ‏כְּתָב‎ script. This script is based on the lettering used by many medieval *so-frim* (mainly in Central Europe) when they wrote documents other than the Torah, *tefillin*, or *mezuzah*. It requires much practice to master. The basic line is three nib-units high, with two nib-units for descenders and two nib-units for the ascender, *lamed*. The nib is most often held at a 90° angle (the same as that of nib-units). Nib angle is *changed*, however, to approximately 60° when making the diamond-shaped vertical strokes. (Make these strokes by placing the right edge of the nib on the vertical line left by the *yod*, the basis for most letters, then move the nib diagonally downward toward the right. Stop when the left edge of the nib reaches the bottom of the three-nib-unit line and is directly below the vertical line at the same time.) The descending strokes in the final forms and *kof* are begun with the nib at a 60° angle. As you move the pen downward, rotate the nib so that its angle becomes 90°.

Rashi script. This script is based on the script used for most Rabbinical commentaries. It is called ‎רש״י‎ [*Rashi*] because the first commentaries to be published in this script were written by *Rabbi Shlomo Yitzḥaki* (acronym, *Rashi*), one of the greatest and best-known Rabbis in Jewish history. It requires many different nib angles, the most dominant being close to 90°. The basic line is four nib-units, with two nib-units for descenders and two nib-units for ascenders (*lamed* and *tzaddi*).

III

DEVELOPING AN ILLUMINATED MANUSCRIPT

1
After the Plates

Once you've mastered the plates, then what? Practice may make perfect, but just practicing letters all the time can never be a final goal. There comes a time when you must apply the skills you've acquired. No real pianist ever only practiced scales!

What will your first step be? A project. So what's a project? It's the preparation of an "illuminated manuscript," that is, a quotation (your own or one you've found elsewhere) written up with some type of decoration, illustration, or colored border around it.

As you work through the following sections of the book, remember that you're doing something for the first time. Along with the joys and excitement of beginning something new and fresh come the frustrations and difficulties of any beginning skill. (This applies to the plates as well.) Your work won't always come out the perfect way you've pictured it in your mind; these things take time and experience. So don't be overcritical of yourself. Instead, focus on what you're doing and what you're learning in that moment; and enjoy the process itself—your involvement in the activity right now. Enjoy making the individual strokes in the letters. Meditate upon the quotation to which you're about to devote so much time and thought. Picture the illumination you'll use. You can even take pleasure in the fact that you're learning from your own mistakes as you proceed. Of course, you want to produce something, and you want it to be beautiful—but if you put your trust in the process, the product will appear.

TOOLS AND MATERIALS

The materials you will need in order to execute your project will vary greatly according to the type of presentation you want. The list below does not pretend to be all-inclusive, but it does name most of the basic materials that you will want to make use of in developing a quotation for presentation, especially with illumination.

Bristol paper pad, with a vellum or kid finish (9" x 12" or 11" x 14").
   This paper is thick paper. The smaller size should be adequate for a first project, but many stationery and art stores only carry the larger size. Vellum or kid means that the surface is slightly rough, has some "tooth" to it. This provides the friction necessary to draw ink out of the pen when the nib is drawn over it. You don't want a surface with a "high" or "plate" finish. In that case the pen will glide along the surface with much less control on your part.
   When you move on to more ambitious projects, you may want to invest in large sheets of 100% cotton paper. There are many fine brands such as Strathmore, Rives, Arches, Fabiano, and Bainbridge, as well as many excellent handmade papers. The importance of 100% cotton is that the paper will last a long time (under good conditions) without yellowing or deteriorating.

Tracing paper pad, 9" x 12".
   Since I use tracing paper to transfer designs and as protective coverings for both work in process and on finished work, I buy the cheapest available. (See pp. 116 and 119 for more detailed discussion.)

Drafting tape.
   No, it's not masking tape, though it looks like it. The difference is that drafting tape doesn't tear your paper when it is removed. It comes in small tape dispensers or larger rolls. It also comes in various widths; I find ¾" wide tape to be the most convenient.

6B, 5B, or 4B pencil.
Try to get the softest, 6B, if you can. This pencil will be used in transferring designs onto the manuscript.

9H, 8H, or 7H pencil.
A very hard pencil, 9H being the hardest. This will be used for drawing guidelines and transferring designs.

HB pencil.
You should already have this (see p. 5).

Erasing shield.
This is a wonderful device, made to protect areas you don't want the eraser to touch. Shields come in various sizes and are made up of any of a number of materials. I prefer metal and the smallest size (about 2½″ x 3¾″), as seen in figure 40 on p. 115. (See p. 115 for more on its use.)

Typewriter eraser (an ink eraser).
The kind I like best is a hard, pink or gray circle of rubber attached to a little brush (see figure 40 on p. 115). I prefer the circular kind to the ones that look like a pencil, or those that are shaped like an oblong parallelogram. If you decide to devote a lot of your time to calligraphy, you might eventually invest in an electric eraser, a wonderful labor-saving device.

Single-edged razor blade.
This has only one sharp edge; the other edge has a piece of metal as a safety guard.

Kneaded eraser.
This is very useful for cleaning and for erasing pencil lines. It doesn't leave pieces of eraser and is practically self-cleaning.

Cotton balls.
For use in removing excess graphite from the tracing paper when preparing to transfer a design. See the section on the transfer of designs, p. 119.

Small can, jar, cup, or plastic container that will hold a decent amount of water (5 to 10 ounces or so).

Ruling pen.
See p. 129 for a detailed explanation.

Compass.
See p. 131.

French curve(s).
This will be discussed in the section "Writing on a Curve" on p. 131.

(Materials like watercolors, gouache, brushes, palette, and gold ink will be discussed in the sections on "Illuminating the Manuscript.")

2

The Manuscript

CHOOSING A TEXT

The text you choose to work on may be anything from a Biblical quotation to a verse from modern Yiddish or Hebrew poetry. It may be from the Talmud or from other traditional texts such as the *Siddur* (the prayer book), the *Haggadah* (the Passover text), or books of midrashim; or it may be something from any language that you or someone you know can translate into Hebrew.

Once you've found a text, you need to design an illumination that is compatible with (or expressive of) the words you've chosen. Whatever text you choose will probably suggest an appropriate design, be it a literal expression or a more abstract one. (See page 117 for some suggestions and examples.)

For a first project, keep your ambitions modest. This is not yet the time to tackle a *ketubah* (a Jewish marriage document), even though your cousin is getting married in three weeks. Pick a quotation that is not too long; ten to twenty words should be sufficient.

A NOTE ON BIBLICAL VERSES
Biblical verses, especially those from the Torah (the first five books,

often called the Five Books of Moses) are not only written with vowels and *dageshim* (dots in the centers of letters), but also with diacritical marks that indicate the cantillation, a way of chanting or singing the verse. This is called the *trop*. There may also be dashes in verses, and there are two dots (like a colon) at the end of each verse. (See figure 34.)

וַאֲכַלְתֶּם אֹתוֹ בְּכָל־מָקוֹם אַתֶּם וּבֵיתְכֶם כִּי־שָׂכָר הוּא

לָכֶם חֵלֶף עֲבֹדַתְכֶם בְּאֹהֶל מוֹעֵד: וְלֹא־תִשְׂאוּ עָלָיו

חֵטְא בַּהֲרִימְכֶם אֶת־חֶלְבּוֹ מִמֶּנּוּ וְאֶת־קָדְשֵׁי בְנֵי־יִשְׂרָאֵל

לֹא תְחַלְּלוּ וְלֹא תָמוּתוּ:

Fig. 34. Biblical verse, showing *trop*.

When copying such texts, only write the letters, and leave out all of these marks. (You may wish to retain the colon indicating the end of a verse, but I delete it.) If you feel it absolutely necessary to include vowels, make them with a pointed pen (such as a felt-tip or plastic-point marker). Vowels are not easily made with a broad-nibbed pen; when done so, they are often out of scale to the letters.

MUCH PLANNING—EASY PROJECT

The more carefully you organize your quotation and design before you set it up on good paper, the better it will look, and the less will go wrong with it. Careful planning also means fewer errors, less uncertainty, less of a feeling of pressure when you get to the final draft. The way to accomplish this is to go through the process of layout.

LAYOUT

Choosing a layout means making a series of decisions. Sketch out everything in rough form at first (on graph paper) and see what questions arise as you work. Should the paper be placed vertically or horizontally? Where should the quotation be placed? How should the words be phrased? Does the spacing make it easy to read and fit on the page well? How do the design and quotation relate to each other? Have a fair number of different layouts been tried?

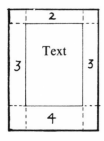

Fig. 35. Margins. These are "classic" proportions for a manuscript page, detailing margins and the area of the text in relation to the total area of the page.

MARGINS

There are "classic" proportions for a page, regulating what area should be taken up by the manuscript and what margins should be left on top, on the bottom, and on the sides (see figure 35). (In a manuscript book the margin closest to the spine of the book will be different than the margin on the other side.) Two good expositions of this will be found in the books *Writing & Illuminating & Lettering* by Edward Johnston (Chapter VI, Manuscript Books) and *The Calligrapher's Handbook,* edited by C. M. Lamb (Chapter VII, The Design of Manuscript Books and Inscriptions by M. C. Oliver). (See the bibliography.)

In general, you will probably want to place your quotation so that the top margin is smaller than the bottom, perhaps in a ratio of 2:3 or 2½:3. Try to work out your margins so that the calligraphy and the illumination together take up an area a little more than half the area of the paper. If the area of the paper is 100 square inches, you might want your illuminated manuscript to take up 52 square inches.

This brings us to the size of the paper. Should it be 8" x 10", 9" x 12", 11" x 14"? This all depends upon how much space you need or want in order to present your idea. Will there be a lot of illumination? Will there be a lot of space between the quotation and the illumination? Do you want a tight-looking piece or one that has lots of "air?"

LAYOUT POSSIBILITIES

There are many options for the arrangement of a quotation on paper (see figure 36). You may want the quotation to be in one line (1), or broken up into two or three lines (2). You may want your quotation "flush right"—justified at the right (3), with the left margin unjustified so that your design can go there. Or you may want the border design on the right, in which case the quotation will go flush left, with the right text margin unjustified (4).

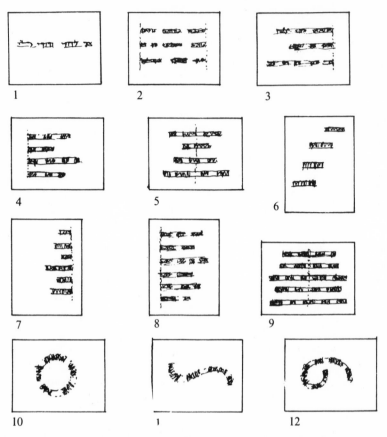

Fig. 36. Layout possibilities. These are different possibilities for the layout of a quotation on a page: 1) The words all in one line. 2) Two or three lines of manuscript, justified both right and left. 3) The text justified right. 4) The text justified left. 5) The text centered. 6) The words diagonally staggered down the page. 7) Placement of one word per line (in this case justified right). 8) Manuscript placed phrase by phrase (in this case justified left). 9) The text written line by line (in this case centered). 10) Writing the text in a circle. 11) Writing the text in a curve. 12) Writing the text in a spiral.

The quotation can be symmetrically balanced in the center of the paper (5), or staggered diagonally down the page (6). You may want to break up the text word by word (7), phrase by phrase (8), or line by line (9). How you will place your quotation on the paper will depend upon the length, phrasing, and the visual expression that you want to present in your project. The quotation might even be written in a circle (10), a curve (11), or a spiral (12). (See the section dealing with "Writing on a Curve," page 131.)

No one layout is the "correct" one; there are many creative ways in which a quotation may be presented. But it is useful to see the options so that you can make your choice clearly.

One helpful method of choosing your layout is to write out the text of your quotation on graph paper, in whatever script you have chosen. Cut out the individual words, and arrange them on another piece of paper to see what the different possibilities might look like.

(Remember to follow the requirements of spacing we have discussed. Leave at lease five nib-units between lines, though you may find it more aesthetically pleasing to leave more space, say, ten nib-units.)

JUSTIFYING A LINE

Occasionally the need arises to line up, or justify, *both* the right- and left-hand margins of a text. If you look at a typewritten page, you will notice that while the left margin is almost always even, the right margin is often uneven, or unjustified. A look at any newspaper column or book, on the other hand, will show that both the right and left margins are justified. Printers do this by stretching the type evenly, with a little extra—and equal—space between each letter, or between words. For this reason, some lines may look dense or tight, while others appear more open.

Even though this method may be used to justify a line when writing a manuscript in calligraphy, it generally looks better to keep your letters and words spaced tightly and let only a few letters be stretched.

LETTERS THAT CAN BE USED IN JUSTIFYING A LINE
Those letters in the Hebrew alphabet that have a horizontal stroke at the top of the three-nib-unit line may be extended horizontally if necessary to justify a line. This basic principle holds only as long as the extension of the horizontal stroke does not violate the intrinsic characteristic of the letter. For example, the extension of the horizontal element of a *vav* would change that letter into a *resh*. Or the extension of the horizontal element of a final *nun* would convert it into a final *khaf*. This principle is valid if the letter has a horizontal stroke only at the

Fig. 37. Letters that can be used in justifying a line. These letters may be elongated horizontally when necessary (or desirable) to justify a line. *Lamed* and *kof* should only be elongated when no other letters are available.

top of the three-nib-unit line, but not also one at the bottom. Extension of both the top and bottom horizontal elements, as in the letters *fe* or final *mem*, would make the letters look extremely heavy. So the letters I recommend extending when justification of a line is desired are: *dalet, he, ḥet, khaf sofit, fe sofit, resh,* and *tav.* In addition, *lamed* and *kof* are possibilities, but I suggest using them only when there are no other letters available that can be extended (see figure 37). This only applies to the basic script in the plates. Letters used in justifying a line for other scripts are noted on the page of each script.

DRAFTING TECHNIQUES

Once you've decided on a layout for your text, have done a few rough drafts of it on graph paper, and have chosen the illumination and where it will go on the manuscript (see the sections on "Illumination"), you are ready to begin the final draft on the bristol paper (or whatever paper you have chosen). You need to place the paper down on your table or drafting board and prepare it for the actual writing of the text. Some drafting techniques and a few tools used in drafting will be extremely helpful at this point.

T-SQUARE AND TRIANGLE
A T-square is called that because it is in the shape of a *T,* and forms a "square," or right angle, at the crossbar. It is useful because you can draw parallel lines with it. All you need is a table that has one true edge (smooth and straight). As you slide the crossbar along that edge,

each line made by the long part will be parallel to any other line. The T-square is of even greater usefulness when used in conjunction with a triangle. (See figure 38.)

T-squares are made of many different materials: wood, plastic (or acrylic), wood-and-plastic combination, aluminum, single-weight steel, and double-weight steel. Wood is light and relatively inexpensive, but tends to warp, and pieces of wood can splinter from the edges. Plastic is cheap, but less true and straight, and can easily scratch and warp. Wood-and-plastic does not warp so easily, but may break at the juncture of the wood and the plastic. Aluminum is lightweight, but warps easily. Single-weight steel is heavy and costly, and can warp. Double-weight steel warps very little, but is heavy and very expensive. T-squares are available in lengths from 12″ to 48″ (4 feet) and up. I use one 30″ in length, but a shorter one may well meet your needs at first.

Triangles used with T-squares basically come in two forms. Both are right triangles, but one is a right isosceles triangle (90°–45°–45°); the other has 30° and 60° angles. (You can also purchase "adjustable"

Fig. 38. T-square and triangles (45°–45°–90° triangle and 30°–60°–90° triangle). The cross-bar of the T-square is placed along the true edge on the left side of the drawing board or table. If left-handed, place the T-square with the cross-bar along a true edge on the right edge of the board or table. Triangles should be placed with the right angle on the left (as seen with the 30°–60°–90° triangle) for the right-handed. If left-handed, place the triangle with the right angle on the right (as seen with the 45°–45°–90° triangle).

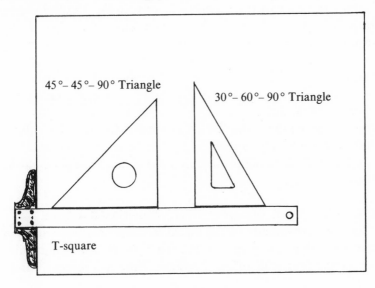

45°– 45°– 90° Triangle

30°– 60°– 90° Triangle

T-square

triangles, so called because you can change the angle to any one desired; but I'll limit my discussion to the two I have mentioned.)

When a triangle is placed along the edge of the long part of the T-square, it insures that any line drawn along the edge of that triangle will be parallel to all the lines drawn with that same edge of that same triangle. This combined use of T-square and triangle makes measuring a page for layout easier, and minimizes error.

The possibilities of the T-square and triangle are expanded when one realizes that not only can one make parallel vertical and horizontal lines, and lines that are parallel at 60°, 30°, and 45°, but one can also make lines that are parallel at 75° and 15°, by combining the two triangles.

Some people put pennies or thicknesses of tape underneath the T-square, so that it slides more easily on the board and over the paper. But I find that this raises the T-square too high above the surface of the paper. And the pennies and tape tend to pick up dirt which is easily transferred to the paper.

The correct way to move a T-square—the way that poses the least risk of smudging your work—is to lift the T-square off the board (and paper) by using the crossbar as a lever and slide the crossbar along the edge of the board (or table) until the T-square is in the desired position. Release the leverage and let the long edge slowly down until it rests on the paper. Move a triangle in the same way: Lift it by its corner so that only the edge of the triangle adjacent to the T-square remains on the paper (or board). Slide the triangle along the edge of the T-square until it is in the desired position, and then lower the triangle.

If you are right-handed, everything should be placed to your left. The true edge should be the left edge of the table or board, the crossbar should be at that true edge, and your light source should be at the upper left-hand corner.

If you're left-handed, the T-square should be placed so that the crossbar is at your right, along the true edge at the right side of the table or board. And the light source should be at the upper right-hand corner of your table.

TAPING THE PAPER DOWN ON THE BOARD OR TABLE
With the T-square already on the board, and the crossbar snug against the true edge, place the paper so that the bottom edge is immediately adjacent to the long edge of the T-square. Take two pieces of drafting

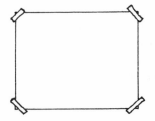

Fig. 39. Taping the paper down. The tape is placed diagonally, exposing the corners so that accurate measurements can be made.

tape, each about two and a half inches long, and tape down the two top corners of the paper. Place each piece of tape *across* each corner (as in a photo album), leaving a little of each corner visible. Lower the T-square from the bottom edge of the paper, and tape the two bottom corners in the same manner. This locks the paper into a secure position. Check your alignment (assuming the piece of paper is itself square) by taking a triangle, and with one edge of the right angle against the long edge of the T-square, see if the other side of the right angle of the triangle lines up with the perpendicular edges of the paper. (See figure 39.)

MEASURING ON THE PAPER

After you've determined the exact placement of your text on the paper—the length of each line, the spacing between lines, and the margins—draw pencil lines to indicate these measurements. These pencil lines act as guidelines for the lettering (the three-nib-unit line) and for the placement of your design. Accurate measurement of these pencil lines insures that your work will look clean and neat.

Measuring is always done by placing a ruler (or architect's scale) along a true edge (which can be the edge of the paper—left or right sides, top or bottom), or along a line parallel to a true edge (made with T-square or T-square and triangle). Always measure by looking from directly above the points you are measuring. The first measurement is always made along the edge of the paper, then a parallel line can be drawn using T-square or T-square and triangle from the point measured. Placing the drafting tape so that the corners of the paper are visible allows the first measurement (from one corner of the paper and along an edge of the paper) to be accurate.

Each measurement should be indicated by a point; pencil lines are then drawn from the points measured. Make all points and pencil lines using a hard pencil (like a 9H). Hold the pencil just as you hold the pen. Place the pencil point against the edge of the T-square or the triangle. Draw the pencil from left to right (for the T-square) or from bottom to top (for the triangle) along this edge. (The triangle is usually placed so that the right angle is on the left.)

If you are left-handed, draw the pencil from right to left along the T-square or from bottom to top along the edge of the triangle (placed with the right angle on the right).

Always press lightly with the pencil. This insures light guidelines (which require less erasing) and no indentation on the paper from the hard point.

WRITING THE TEXT

With your paper taped down and all your guidelines measured and drawn, you are ready to letter your text. Take a clean piece of paper and place it on the lined paper just below the first set of guidelines. This will keep the oils in your hand from getting on the paper; it will also focus your attention on the line you are lettering.

Write out the first line carefully, making continual reference to the first line of your rough draft. Move the paper down line by line until the text is finished.

AVOIDING ERRORS IN THE TEXT

The errors that are sometimes made in transcribing a text can be frustrating and time-consuming. Since so much effort and preparation has been put into your work so far, you'll want the first attempt not to be wasted. To protect your project from the danger of errors, check the rough draft of your text over carefully before copying it onto good paper. Study it so that you clearly see its phrases, their lengths, and the spelling of the words.

There are common scribal errors to watch for. One is the *homoteleuton*, from two Greek words meaning "same word." Let's assume, for example, that you are copying the text "Now is the time for all good people to come to the aid of their country." You've begun copying the first line and it looks like this:

NOW IS THE

Your eye goes back to where you left off, at the word "the." But instead of looking at the phrase "Now is the time," your eye falls on the second "the" in the sentence, found in the phrase "come to the aid." Before you realize that anything is wrong, you've written:

NOW IS THE AID OF THEIR COUNTRY

Another example of a *homoteleuton:* You've chosen a selection from Chapter I, verse 2 of *Pirkei Avot* [Ethics of the Fathers]. It reads: ·

עַל שְׁלֹשָׁה דְבָרִים

הָעוֹלָם עוֹמֵד

עַל הַתּוֹרָה

וְעַל הָעֲבוֹדָה

וְעַל גְּמִילוּת חֲסָדִים

[Upon three things the world is based: upon the Torah, upon Divine service, and upon the doing of good deeds.] You've copied the opening statement; it looks like this:

עַל שְׁלֹשָׁה דְבָרִים

הָעוֹלָם עוֹמֵד

You copy the next line, the first of the three items. Now your paper looks like this:

עַל הַתּוֹרָה

You continue copying. Something distracts you, or perhaps your eyes are tired, but your eye catches

ועל

[and upon] in the third line, instead of in the second, and your work ends up with a line missing:

על שלשה דברים

העולם עומד

על התורה

ועל גמילות חסדים

Two other common scribal errors to avoid are the dittograph and the haplograph. Dittography is the unintentional repetition of a letter or word. This often occurs at the juncture of two lines. One writes a word at the end of a line, then unintentionally writes the same word at the beginning of the next line.

Haplography, the opposite of dittography, is the telescoping of two words into one. Suppose you were copying שלום ולהתראות [Goodbye until I see you again]. You've copied the three letters של and somehow your eye picks up the second ו (vav) in ולהתראות and you start copying from there. You arrive at שלות.

When doing calligraphy, *never assume you know how to spell.* This can be doubly helpful when copying from the Bible, where often the same Hebrew words are spelled differently in different places. A simple example is

ירושלים

[Jerusalem]. Today it is spelled in this way. But in many places in the Bible (such as in the Psalms), it is spelled

(omitting the *yod*).

Certain words are pronounced differently than they are written in the Bible. The word as it is written is called the *k'tib*, the way it is to be pronounced is called the *k'ray*. The Masoretes annotated certain words in this way to indicate the opinion that errors may have been made by scribes when transcribing those words. Every word in the Bible is considered sacred, and not to be changed, so this system was instituted for those words. The *k'ray* is usually denoted in the margin or as a note at the bottom of the page in most Hebrew Bibles. An example appears in Jeremiah 9:7. The *k'tib* is שוחט, which might be pronounced *shohet*, and would mean "slaughters," or "the slaughterer." The *k'ray* is שחוט, which is to be pronounced *shahoot*, and can mean "slaughtered," "sharpened," or "hammered, beaten." The first three words of the verse in Jeremiah are חץ שחוט לשונם and are usually translated "their tongue is a sharpened arrow," based on the *k'ray*. You should probably use the *k'ray* when transcribing the text, but be aware that you are then changing the text.

Another way to avoid errors is: *Never assume you know anything from memory.* When copying a text, always have it directly in front of you. Use a piece of paper or a ruler to cover the line above and below the line you are copying, so that only that line is visible. Check and re-check the text. Know it intimately. After every word or two, check yourself. Say the word or letters out loud as you copy. Use any and all means to make sure you are faithful to the text.

CORRECTING ERRORS IN THE TEXT
Unfortunately, no matter how careful you are, every so often you'll make an error. You'll discover a letter left out, a misspelled word, a dittograph or a haplograph, or even (heaven forfend!) a *homoteleuton*. What happens? Usually anger, frustration, panic. . . . What to do?

The first thing is to calm down so that you can make an accurate assessment of the situation. So take a little break. Get something to drink. Read. Listen to some music. Go for a walk. Rant and rave for a little bit. The calligrapher's maxim, in other words, is: Never try to correct an error while the ink is still wet. Leave it alone until you can see objectively what must be done.

How bad is it? You've left out a whole line, or three lines, or repeated a whole phrase. Sometimes, you actually have to start over again. Sadly, you lift the paper off the board. But don't throw it out. You've gained some knowledge from your mistake. You know how to be more careful in the planning and the copying the next time. You know not to try to rush things or work under pressure. And you have a very good idea of the spacing of the letters, words, and phrases you did correctly, so that the second attempt will be perfect.

But what if you discover the error as soon as it's made? You've just repeated a letter. Or you wrote the wrong letter. Or you realize immediately that you've left out a word. Suppose you were using as your text this verse from Ecclesiastes 1:9:

ואין כל חדש תחת השמש

[. . . And there is nothing new under the sun.] And instead of copying it correctly, you wrote

ואין כל תחת

and immediately realized the error of your ways. If you realize it quickly enough, take a tissue and blot out the incorrect word immediately. This keeps the ink from seeping into the paper, and makes correction easier.

Now let's assess the error. You need to erase **תחת**

and put **חדש**

in its place. Look at the words letter by letter. Since a **ח** (*ḥet*) must replace a **ת** (*tav*) and since they are very similarly formed, it is only necessary to replace the left side of the *tav*. The **ח** (*ḥet*), being replaced by a **ד** (*dalet*), will need to be erased only in the upper right-hand corner (or not at all, if you've chosen the squared-off option for your letters). The **ת** (*tav*), however, will need to be completely erased, since it shares no intrinsic characteristics with the **ש** (*shin*).

Begin the correcting procedure. Place tracing paper down to keep the oils and sweat from your hand from affecting the paper. Leave the area to be corrected uncovered. Take a single-edged razor blade (see figure 40), and holding the edge of the blade as closely parallel to the

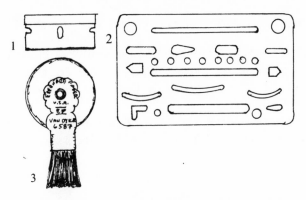

Fig. 40. Erasing kit. 1) Single–edged razor blade. 2) Erasing shield. 3) Typewriter eraser.

surface of the paper as possible, lightly scrape away with a corner at the surface ink on the sections to be erased. Scrape too deeply and you'll find a nice little hole in your paper.

Now take the erasing shield (see figure 40) and place the smallest opening possible to go over the area being corrected. Correct only small areas at a time. Take your ink eraser (the round typewriter eraser with the brush, shown in figure 40) and rub vigorously over the area visible through the opening in the erasing shield. Using a light brush or light clean rag, brush away the pieces of eraser and see if all the ink has been erased. Do not blow away the erasure with your breath; you may make the situation worse with drops of saliva. And don't brush it away with your hand. The natural oils of the body can affect the paper adversely. Repeat the procedure until all the ink has been removed from that area.

When all of the ink has been erased from that area, go on to the next, select a suitable opening in the erasing shield, and erase some more. Keep working at it until all erasures have been made.

If you find yourself getting tired by all this hard erasing, you might think about buying an electric eraser. It does most of the erasing for you, and most models feature a variety of points for different kinds of erasing—pencil, ink, etc. The investment is well worth it. The razor blade must still be used, however.

After all the erasing has been completed and the paper is clean and free of eraser pieces, take a good look to make sure you've gotten *all* of the ink erased. Sometimes it's helpful to use the razor blade again, but this tends to make the paper a bit rough. As a matter of fact erasing itself makes the paper a bit rough, and rough paper tends to bleed—

that is, the ink tends to feather, as though you were putting a felt-tip pen to a very porous paper like a napkin or tissue. So smooth the paper down by pounding the paper lightly with a kneaded eraser. Do this with firm hard motions.

Once the paper is smooth, you can write in the correct letters or parts of letters. Be careful to write lightly. And for God's sake, don't make a mistake.

INSURANCE AND PROTECTION

Once you've done the calligraphy and are ready to begin work on the illumination, cut a piece of tracing paper exactly to the shape of the quotation, and tape it lightly over the text with small pieces of drafting tape in order to protect the work from being damaged by smudges or an accidental drop of paint.

3

Illuminating
the Manuscript

ILLUMINATION CHOICES

The patterns and designs, colors and pictures, and/or brilliance of gold
that constitute illumination can add wonderful dimensions to any
manuscript. Of course, the calligraphy and the layout of a quotation—
that is, the sheer visual effect of a manuscript—can be beautiful by itself, without illumination. Whether or not to use illumination is a
question you will have to consider anew for each project. On the other
hand, the illumination can be as simple as a border line running
alongside the calligraphy, or a rubric (an illuminated letter or word).

What is the appropriate visual expression for a quotation? Suppose
you've chosen to write out the first line of the Torah (Genesis 1:1):

בראשית ברא אלר־ים

את השמים ואת האר־ץ

[In the beginning, God created the heavens and the earth.] Some possibilities might be the color of the sky above the text and an earth color below. Or a rainbow. Or a beautiful floral border.

Suppose you chose these verses from Song of Songs 2:10–12:

קומי לך רעיתי

יפתי ולכי לך

כי הגה הסתו עבר

הגשם חלף הלך לו

הנצנים נראו בארץ

עת הזמיר הגיע

וקול התור נשמע בארצו

[Arise, my beloved, my beautiful one, come away! For now the winter is past, the rains are over and gone. The blossoms have appeared in the land, the time of singing has come, the voice of the dove is heard in our land.] An appropriate illumination for this text might be based on a pattern of blossoms and leaves, doves, and musical notes or instruments.

Some texts may not suggest such literal illumination interpretation. An abstract pattern might be a better choice for many texts. Such designs can be found everywhere. Chances are that some item from your wardrobe has a design that you would like to adapt for a project. Of course, any number of books with designs in them can provide you with ideas. (Two wonderful books are *Hebrew Illuminated Manuscripts* and *The Ketuba: Jewish Marriage Contracts through the Ages,* discussed in the bibliography; another excellent source series is the great variety of Dover books of patterns, designs, etc.) But I've also found designs on walls in coffee shops, on building facades, almost everywhere. You might start keeping a file of illumination ideas—pictures of birds, flower catalogs, geometric patterns, oriental rug designs, and so forth.

TRANSFERRING DESIGNS

Once you have a design, you'll need to transfer it onto the paper containing your chosen text. The method described here is only useful when the design you're transferring is going to remain the same size on your project.

Take a piece of tracing paper and place it on the design to be transferred. Tape it down using drafting tape (or pin it if on cloth), so that it will remain stationary. Then, using an HB pencil, trace the design carefully. Remove the tracing paper and turn it over so that the traced design is on the obverse. Now take a 6B pencil (very soft) and rub the graphite from the pencil over the area taken up by the design. Rub the graphite smooth using a cotton ball, and thus prevent excess graphite from making your fingers or the paper with your text dirty. Now turn the paper over again so that the side with the traced design faces up, and position it on the paper with your text. The advantage of using tracing paper for this process is that you can see through it, and so get a good idea of how the design will look in relation to the calligraphy. Take a very hard pencil (9H, 8H, or 7H) and retrace the design, being careful not to press too hard. Pressing too hard will cause an indentation in the paper receiving the design, and may also cut the tracing paper. Be sure to retrace the entire design. Then remove the tracing paper, and your design is ready to be colored in. Since graphite (rather than the carbon of carbon paper) was the transfer material, any or all of it can be erased.

COLOR

Color, as part of illumination, adds vibrance and vitality to any design around a manuscript. The subtlety or extravagance with which color can be used, plus the very wide range of different colors available, create almost endless possibilities for illuminating a text.

Coloring material comes in many different forms—powder, tubes, cake, liquid—and media—oil paints, acrylic paints, oil pastels, charcoal pastels, watercolor, gouache, and others.

I will confine my remarks here to watercolor and gouache. Oil is not useful for illumination because it tends to dissolve paper. I find that acrylic dries too quickly and is too thick. Pastels are highly susceptible to smudging. Watercolor and gouache have none of these disadvantages and yet have a rich and subtle effect. Moreover, they are easier to work with.

Watercolor is coloring material that is diluted with water, usually to produce more or less translucent coloring (depending upon the amount of water used to dilute the watercolor). Gouache is watercolor that has had honey and gum arabic added to give the color an opaque quality and some substance.

You can purchase watercolor in cakes, tubes, or bottles. (Powder must be mixed with other material before it can be used, and so will not be discussed.) Watercolor in cakes is watercolor in its most solid form. Simply add a few drops of water either to the cake or to the brush and it is ready to use. Watercolor in tubes is material in a concentrated form, which you can dilute with water to any thickness you like. When placed on a palette, it will dry in time, but can be reused by the addition of water. (When you purchase watercolors consider buying a palette—a portable, flat (though some have shallow depressions) surface upon which to place, mix, and store your watercolors or gouache after they have been removed from the tubes.) You can store watercolor or gouache after they have dried for an indefinite period as long as the paint is covered with plastic wrap or aluminum foil to keep it free of dust. Watercolor in bottles has already been diluted a great deal, and is watercolor in its most liquid form. It is quite translucent, which makes it very useful for washes and light effects but it cannot be made thicker or less translucent. Bottled watercolors can also be used as colored inks.

Gouache is usually only available in tubes. It is also thinned with water, but tends to stay opaque (when dry). Its advantage, aside from the richness and creaminess of its effect, is that it can be "overpainted"—that is, once one color (say red) is painted, another color (say yellow) can be painted on top of the first color, without the two colors blending (to form orange), which is what would happen with watercolor. Of course, the first color should be dry, and the second color not too diluted.

Some useful basic colors are: Ultramarine, Alizarin Crimson, Permanent Green, Spectrum Yellow, Burnt (or Raw) Sienna (or Umber),

Yellow Ochre, Ivory (or Jet) Black, Chinese (also called Zinc) White.

There are many different brands of watercolors. Cakes are made by Winsor and Newton, Grumbacher, Guitar, and numerous other companies. Tubes are made by Winsor and Newton, Grumbacher, and others. Bottled watercolors are produced by Luma and Dr. Martin's. Gouache is made by Winsor and Newton, and Grumbacher.

USE OF WATERCOLOR AND GOUACHE

I use distilled water to thin watercolor or gouache because it is free of trace minerals which might affect the paint. (I still have the same gallon I bought many years ago.) I pour off water into a smaller bottle with a cap that can be adjusted to release one drop of water at a time. You might also use a medicine dropper to control the precise amount of water you add to the paint; or you can dip a narrow brush into a cup of water and add a drop at a time to the paint in this way.

If you are using tubes, squeeze a small amount from the tube onto the palette. If you need to mix two or more colors, squeeze the necessary amount of each color on a different part of the palette, but near each other. (As anyone knows who has ever painted a house with mixed paint and tried to match it later, it pays to squeeze out a little more than you think you'll need.) If using cakes, you can use them in the tins provided. Bottled watercolors can be used with the dropper provided in the bottle.

The cleaning process works as follows: Have three containers of clean water for cleaning your brush between applications of different colors (or when you're finished painting). Container #1 gets the brush straight from the paint. Swirl the brush in the water, cleaning off most of the paint. Then dip the brush into container #2, cleaning the brush further. (The water will be much less dirty.) Finally, dip the brush in container #3. The brush is now almost completely clean, and the water also. Eventually, water will have to be replaced, but less often, and only from one jar at a time. Since container #1 gets dirtiest first, clean it well, add clean water to it, and rename it container #3, turning container #2 into container #1, and container #3 into container #2. (You need not use distilled water for the cleaning process.)

After you've added a drop of water to the paint, take your brush and make the density consistent. Test the paint on a scrap piece of paper (using the same material your text is on). If it is too thick, add another drop of water. If it is too thin, let it evaporate for a few minutes, and test the density again. Painting a small amount on a scrap piece of paper also allows you to see the colors when dry, and to experiment with different combinations and color schemes.

Experiment a little with the density and ways of using paint and manipulating the brush. Think of the colors you might use to paint your illumination and try different combinations. Get a book or two out of the library on watercolor techniques or on painting. The more you read and experiment, the easier it will be to color your actual project.

BRUSHES

Coloring is best done with brushes made of sable. Sable brushes have fine, flexible bristles that maintain their quality for a long time. The point gives you a fine sharp line or a broad brush stroke, as needed. For illumination work, you will need a few brushes of the smaller sizes, with numbers like 00, 0, or 1. Use watercolor brushes—the shorter ones, not the long ones used for watercolor or acrylic painting. Sable brushes may be more expensive, but cheaper brushes tend to lose hairs, dry with brittle bristles, and don't always come to a precise point.

To get a fine line, hold the brush straight up, perpendicular to the writing surface, with your fingers at the top of the ferrule (the metal part attaching the bristles to the handle). Make sure the brush has been brought to a point, without too much paint on the tip of the brush. Using your last two fingers for support on the paper, put the point of the brush down lightly and draw in the direction of the line. Use smooth longer strokes, rather than short sketchy ones. Even when painting broad areas—where more pressure is applied to the brush to get a broader stroke—try to use the brush smoothly, with confidence, not making short, sketchy strokes.

A LITTLE COLOR THEORY

There are seven (plus two) basic colors in the rainbow: Red, orange, yellow, green, blue, indigo, and violet (which can be remembered by the mnemonic ROY G BIV). White (as in sunlight) is the combination of those seven colors before they get split up by a prism. Black is the (so-called) absence of color. Remember also that there are many different shades of black and white, aside from the shades of gray that occur from the different mixtures of black and white.

If we put the three primary colors—red, yellow, blue—into a triangular configuration, we get a better idea of how to achieve secondary and tertiary colors. Secondary colors are the result of mixing two primaries. Tertiary colors are the result of mixing a primary and a secondary color adjacent to one another. The arrangement of all of these colors as they develop is known as a color wheel (see figure 41).

Other color theory terms are: *value*—refers to the lightness (tint) or darkness (shade) of a color based on the addition of white or black to that color; *hue*—the amount of pure color; *wash*—the dilution of the strength of a color by the continual addition of water; *chroma*—the grayness of a color.

PAINTING TECHNIQUES

You've written out your text, protectively covered it with tracing paper, and drawn (or transferred) your design on the paper. Now it's time to begin painting the illumination. Always paint slowly and carefully.

There are different techniques that can be used in painting. In general, to fill in a number of colors on an illumination design, my suggestion is to start with the lighter colors and work your way up to the darker ones. This means, for example, starting with all the yellow sections, then moving from there on to orange, red, green, blue, violet. (This technique is not always to be used. When painting a vine with flowers, for example, you'll probably want to paint the vine—green—

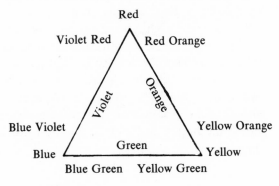

Fig. 41. A little color theory.

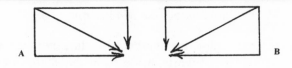

Fig. 42. Direction of painting. a) For the right–handed. b) For the left–handed.

first.) Begin painting from the upper left-hand corner of your paper and move toward the lower right-hand corner (as in figure 42). (If you are left-handed, paint from the upper right-hand corner toward the lower left-hand corner.) This insures that you will not place your hand over previously painted sections, and prevents smudging. Use tracing paper here also as a protection against the oils and sweat in your hand.

If you are using watercolor, remember that it's not easy to overpaint one color on top of another without getting a mix of two colors. For example, painting yellow on top of red will sometimes give you orange. Whether the colors mix depend upon how wet the colors are (particularly the second color added). Sometimes mixing can be prevented by making sure the second color is relatively dry.

You may deliberately choose to let the two colors mix. For example, you may want pink to be the final color. So paint your first color red, then paint white, and you'll get pink.

Gouache is particularly useful in preventing mixtures of two colors when one is overpainted on the other because of its richness and opacity. It's still important that the paint not be too wet in the second color.

Colors can also be mixed to obtain the effect of shading, which suggests dimensionality. Shading generally involves the use of at least three colors. One is the base color which is of intermediate value, let's say red (a very useful and pretty color). By adding a slightly darker red—either less diluted, or darkened with black—one can give a shaded effect to the base color, as if it had less light shining on it. Then by adding a lighter red—lightened by white—one can give the effect of a highlight, of light shining on it.

Shading and highlighting can also be accomplished by the addition of slightly wet black or white as the overpainted color. (Sometimes it is desirable to have the first color slightly wet also.) The wetness of the second color combines with the first color to tone it darker (if the second color is black) or lighter (if the second color is white). Shading with gouache is somewhat easier because the color is thicker (as a result of the honey and gum arabic that are added, which also make it opaque).

Let's talk about a few of the specific techniques you might use, say, for painting flowers. Painting primitive flowers is relatively easy. There are many patterns available in books on Indian designs and folk designs, as well as in many of the Dover books. You can paint the flowers very lightly, with small amounts of relatively wet paint (diluted with much water); this will produce a transparent effect. Or you can paint them with lots of paint for a bold effect.

Books on flowers and seed catalogs are two excellent sources for realistic flowers. Impressionistic and expressionistic ways of painting flowers can be found by looking through art books on any of the masters of these styles of painting and seeing what they've done.

Once you have begun to work on flowers, you will need to know how to make a vine. It's important to remember that vines tend to grow in one direction (let's say upward). So let's start our vine by drawing an S curve that keeps winding back and forth (see figure 43). Then, at the tangents (where the curves change direction) make a curve in the same direction, but curving away from the main line. Keep adding tangential curves until you have achieved the density of vine you desire. Remember to keep the vine growing in the same direction. After you have achieved the desired density—or during the process of adding curves—you can add the leaves, either in the shape of teardrops, or the

Fig. 43. Painting a vine.

classical acanthus leaves so often seen in medieval and Renaissance illuminated manuscripts. Remember that leaves alternate from one side of a vine to another.

Now add your flowers. Vary and alternate the forms you've drawn so that they appear in an even and balanced density. Of course, it helps to plan a basic pattern beforehand and paint a section to see how it looks. Try painting the flowers first; or the main vine first, then the flowers, and then the secondary vines.

Many sources for illumination patterns and designs can be found in the books listed in the bibliography. In addition, many facsimiles of illuminated manuscripts are sold in fine art bookstores. Besides *Hebrew Illuminated Manuscripts* and *The Ketuba: Jewish Marriage Contracts through the Ages,* the *Encyclopaedia Judaica* contains color plates and various articles that provide excellent sources for illumination.

RUBRICS

Rubrics are enlarged letters or words that break up the visual effect of a page. (The name comes from the fact that they were originally ruby red in color.) Sometimes a rubric will only occur at the top of the page, sometimes at carefully selected places throughout the text. It can sim-

Fig. 44. Rubric.

ply be an enlarged letter or word, or it can be a letter or word elabo-
rately decorated with colors, miniature pictures, floral patterns, and
gold. An illuminated first word or letter can dramatize a manuscript
very effectively. (See figure 44.)

"Classical" color schemes that are often used are red and gold or
blue and gold, or sometimes violet and gold or reddish orange and
gold. Often there is an overpainting of colors such as white, light blue,
green, or pink to add more contrast to the background color.

Notice that the dominant color is often gold, precious and brilliant,
the unequaled, yet traditional representation of splendor, majesty, and
wealth. Shiny and glorious, it fascinates and enraptures with the
changing effects of light.

You'll find beautiful examples of rubrics in many illuminated manuscripts. See the bibliography for sources.

If you plan to use a rubric, I suggest making a pencil sketch of the
letter and surrounding colors. Painting of the background color should
come first, then the painting of the gold letter or word. (Paint the letter
or word first if the background color is to be gold.) Then paint the bor-
derline around the outside of the decorated area; this encloses and defines the rubric. Finally, do any overpainting, if planned. (See figure
45.)

The gold that is almost universally used in classical illuminated
manuscripts is gold leaf—gold that has been pounded into an ex-

Fig. 45. Painting a rubric. First do the painting of the background color, then the
gold letters.

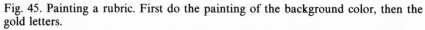

Photo: Bill Aron

tremely thin sheet; it flutters like a butterfly when touched by the slightest breath. Gold leaf is attached to parchment or vellum in most classical manuscripts. Parchment usually refers to the skin of a sheep or goat that has been treated and processed to make it suitable for writing. Vellum is calfskin. Sometimes manuscripts are also written on leather, deerskin, and other animal skins. These skins are the most enduring surfaces to work on. They also have the natural beauty— smoothness, variations in color, small holes, striations and patterns; each piece is unique. Parchment and vellum have come to be interchangeable terms to refer to writing surfaces made from prepared animal skins.

Gold leaf is made to adhere to the parchment by use of a material called a gesso. (Today some gilders use a kind of glue called gold size.) There are many different recipes for gesso (some dating back to the Renaissance). Each ingredient in gesso is included for certain properties: color; creating a hard surface for burnishing the gold and raising it off the paper; and the ability to cause the gold to adhere to it.

Laying gold leaf—gilding—is an art in itself, requiring a great deal of practice, patience, and just the right conditions. It can often be a frustrating and disheartening experience, but one that is more than equaled by the rewards of seeing the beauty of the gold adhering to the gesso and the brilliance of the gold after it has been burnished. If you wish to learn to lay gold leaf, find someone to teach you. You can supplement this instruction by the section on "Gilding" in *The Calligrapher's Handbook* (listed in the bibliography). But be prepared; it is not easy.

One method for giving the appearance of gold (which can't compare to the use of real gold) is to use ersatz gold leaf, made from bronze. It also requires some adhering material, such as gold size or some type of organic glue (seccotine [fish] glue, gum ammoniac, or others, all of which can also be used in laying real gold leaf.)

GOLD INK

A simpler and more easily manageable way of giving the appearance of gold to a manuscript is through the use of gold ink (often made from bronze). Choose a gold ink that is water-based rather than oil-based. Beware of labels that say "CAUTION: Harmful if inhaled or swallowed. Use only in well-ventilated areas. Keep out of the reach of children," and so on. Aside from the health hazards it presents, an oil-based ink will soak through the paper. Use of water-based gold inks also means that washing your brushes and diluting the ink will be relatively easy.

Most gold inks are made from metallic bronze, suspended in a liquid. Since the gold material is relatively heavy, these inks tend to "settle out," leaving the gold material on the bottom and the liquid on the top. Gold ink, when the liquid and metal have been remixed (by following the instructions on the label which tell you to shake well before using), tends to be too thin for rubrics. It does have a shimmering quality that makes it potentially useful as a writing ink, and for such use I would reserve a set of dip pens (but specify them for gold use only, as the gold particles tend to remain even after a good cleaning).

To get the thick, built-up quality preferred for rubrics, I recommend letting the bottle sit for a few days or so until it separates as much as possible. (If it's been sitting in the store for a time, the separation has probably been accomplished, so avoid shaking it up on the way home.) With the gold material settled on the bottom as much as it will, carefully and slowly pour off most of the liquid into another small bottle (reserving it for future use), leaving a thin layer of liquid on top of the gold material to keep it from drying out. Now you're ready to use the gold material in a thickened form. If it's too thick, simply dip the brush in the reserved liquid and add it to the thick gold material until it is diluted enough for your purposes. Dilute the gold material a little at a time as needed. You can always add more liquid, whereas it's harder to take away liquid from a too-thin mixture.

Two brands of gold ink are Winsor and Newton, and Pelikan; there are also cakes of gold color. Though I find Winsor and Newton to be the brightest and most suitable for my needs, the ink made by Pelikan—a little reddish and a bit duller—can be useful when you want to contrast two types of gold. (Gold also comes in powder form, but must be mixed with other materials to be useful and so has not been discussed here.)

USE OF THE RULING PEN

A ruling pen (see figure 46) enables you to make a straight line of constant thickness. It is primarily used not in writing, but for making border lines. A ruling pen works on the principle of capillary action to

Fig. 46. Ruling pen.

hold the ink between the two sides of the pen (which look like tweezers). A tiny screw changes the thickness of the line by increasing or decreasing the space between the two sides of the pen and thereby increasing or decreasing the width of the line of ink that reaches the paper.

To use the ruling pen, make sure the gap between the two sides is not too wide. Then take a medicine dropper or a brush and put a few drops of ink (or liquid watercolors, which often have built-in droppers on their bottles) into the slit through one of the open sides. Too much ink will not be held by the capillary action; too little will necessitate refilling the pen in the middle of making a line.

Test the pen for the desired thickness of line. To make a line, the edge of the pen that is straighter should be placed flat along the edge of the ruling guide (such as a T-square or triangle). Be careful not to place the edge of the ruling pen too close to the edge of the guide, or ink will flow underneath the guide and a smear will result. Keeping this edge of the ruling pen flat (and not allowing it to rotate), pull the pen in the direction of the line desired (as you did when making guidelines with your pencil), keeping your motion constant and the top of the pen tilted in the direction of the motion. A beautiful straight line of constant thickness should result. (Though the ruling pen does require some practice to get used to it, excellent results can be attained.)

If you decide to buy a ruling pen, pay attention to a few details. The two points should meet evenly and be rounded and sharp, not pointy and sharp. If the pen is too sharp it will cut into the paper and will not release ink evenly. One side should be relatively flat, though gently rounded (this is the side to be placed against the ruling guide). The other side should be gently curved. The inside surfaces should be very smooth and flat to hold the ink or liquid watercolor. The adjusting screw should be easy to turn, yet not too loose. A ruling pen can be expensive, so be cautious in purchasing one.

It is also possible to buy a compass with a ruling pen attachment, which enables you to make circles of color for border designs.

The ruling pen is the ancestor of today's "technical fountain pens," such as those made by T-G Castell, Mars, and Rapidograph. These pens are quite useful and have their advantages, but each pen contains a point of only one thickness. Every time you want to change the thickness of line you need to change the point, or use a different pen containing the point of desired thickness. To change the thickness of a line made by the ruling pen, simply turn the adjusting screw. Changes in color in technical fountain pens require washing out the pen completely. A ruling pen, on the other hand, need only be rinsed well and dried. (Like all tools, it should be kept scrupulously clean.) Finally, some technical fountain pens tend to clog; the ink doesn't always flow well.

Technical fountain pens are very useful in graphic design, in touching up work, in making fine lines, and, of course, making lines of a single constant thickness. But ruling pens have none of the difficulties of technical fountain pens and are much easier to use. You also only need one ruling pen.

WRITING ON A CURVE

Curves can either be circles or parts of a circle. These can be made with a compass or a French curve (see figures 47 and 48).

A French curve—actually, there are many kinds of French curves—is an unusually shaped piece of flat transparent plastic perforated with curves over its surface, with no curve being equal to another, nor will any curve maintain the same radius along its length. In other words, the curves change as they continue.

Before you write on a curve, you need to draw guidelines. Pencil in a series of dots on your paper describing the kind of curve you want the

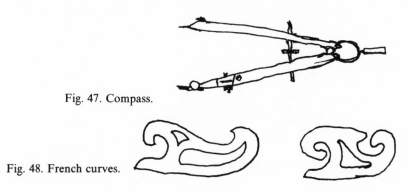

Fig. 47. Compass.

Fig. 48. French curves.

[131]

text to follow. Then, find a curve, or series of curves, on the French curve that nicely fits those points. Draw this curve. Now draw another curve that exactly parallels the first, and is three nib-units away. You can't use the same curve on the French curve to draw both curves, as the second curve will have a different collection of radii than the first. If you plan to write in a circle, draw two circles (three nib-units apart) with a compass.

To write on a curve, you must pretend you are writing on a straight line. Since a curve can be infinitely divided into a series of straight lines, you treat each segment of the curve as a straight line.

Begin to write your text by treating the first part of the curve as a straight line. As you maneuver around the curve, turn the paper so that that part of the curve is a straight line in relation to you. Treat each part of the curve with narrow vision—that is, only look at the segment you are working on—and each part will become a straight line. It is sometimes helpful to draw vertical guidelines at selected points. (These are the radii of the various curves; see figure 49.) Remember to maintain your pen always at the correct angle to that segment of guidelines. When writing long horizontal strokes, follow the curve of the line. Also remember that the top and bottom of your three-nib-unit line (or x-nib-unit line, if doing a script that has different proportional requirements), are of different radii, and therefore, sometimes the letter will look narrower either at the top or at the bottom, depending upon which way the curved lines go.

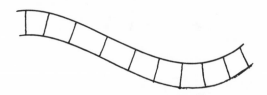

Fig. 49. Guide lines for writing on a curve.

IV
THE ART OF
THE SOFER

The Art of
the Sofer

Throughout this book, I have concentrated on the development of your ability and skill as a calligrapher, from the method of approach to the discussion of the tools and materials to the disciplined practice of the plates, and finally, to the uses to which you can put the skill you have learned. What I have not dealt with (or at least not at any length) is the art of the *sofer,* the classical Jewish scribe, and how this differs from the Hebrew calligraphy you have been learning. Of course, what a *sofer* does is also calligraphy, but more is involved in the structure, standards, and discipline of his work.

A *sofer* must be more than a calligrapher. He must adhere to certain religious standards that have been passed down for thousands of years. This set of standards has usually been called the *halakhah,* which means "the way." It is the system of laws that have been developed by Rabbis throughout the centuries as a guide to the daily conduct of Jews. This system governs every aspect of life, from birth to death. It has been sometimes seen as an evolving system, and much of it is often subject to interpretation. (Who does the interpretation and what kind of interpretation is made has been greatly debated throughout Jewish history and is still debated to this day, especially by the different religious factions in Jewish life.)

The training of a *sofer* usually begins when he is young (though I know many well-trained *sofrim* who began training in adult life) and develops along the lines of an apprentice system. (I refer to a *sofer* as "he" because most *sofrim* are male; I have heard of a *sofer* in Jerusalem who is said to train women as *sofrim,* though this story may be apocryphal. According to some, there are halakhic problems with the training of women as *sofrim.*) This apprentice system is similar to that for the *shohet* (a ritual slaughterer of meat or poultry) or the *mohel* (one who performs the *brit,* the Jewish circumcision ritual). The apprentice trains under one already skilled in the craft until the apprentice gains enough proficiency to perform the craft on his own. This system also can apply to the training of Rabbis. The training is very rigorous and thorough. When one has been trained correctly and satisfactorily, and is deemed worthy of certification by the teacher, one is considered *musmakh,* or "appointed." In this way, the skills and traditions of the craft are carefully passed down from generation to generation. This apprentice system insures that the skill has been scrupulously transmitted, and religious standards are upheld through this form of personal instruction.

A *sofer* should be a religiously observant person. He should follow all the commandments, and be scrupulous in the following of the law. In particular, he must know the laws of his craft extremely well. His religious standards must be the highest, because others depend upon his work for their fulfillment of religious observance. A person who uses a *mezuzah* on his doorpost in keeping with the commandments must rely upon the trustworthiness of the *sofer* who wrote it.

Every morning, as part of the *sofer*'s daily ritual, he will usually immerse himself in a *mikveh,* to insure his purity in preparation for his work. A *mikveh* is a large tub (tall enough to immerse oneself in completely) containing both natural water (rainwater, streamwater, etc.) and processed water (municipal, etc.) that has been mixed according to a prescribed proportion. (A free flowing stream or river may also be used for this ritual immersion.) This immersion, done after the body has already been physically cleansed, cleanses the *sofer* spiritually for his day's work. (There are also some *sofrim* who will immerse themselves in a *mikveh* each time they are about to write God's holy name.)

After the *mikveh,* the *sofer* begins his work by testing his quill to be sure it is properly sharpened. He writes the name עֲמָלֵק (Amalek) and crosses it out, because it is written in the Torah (Deuteronomy

שְׁמַע יִשְׂרָאֵל יְהוָֹה אֱלֹהֵינוּ יְהוָֹה אֶחָד וְאָהַבְתָּ אֵת
יְהוָֹה אֱלֹהֶיךָ בְּכָל לְבָבְךָ וּבְכָל נַפְשְׁךָ וּבְכָל מְאֹדֶךָ וְהָיוּ
הַדְּבָרִים הָאֵלֶּה אֲשֶׁר אָנֹכִי מְצַוְּךָ הַיּוֹם עַל לְבָבֶךָ וְשִׁנַּנְתָּם
לְבָנֶיךָ וְדִבַּרְתָּ בָּם בְּשִׁבְתְּךָ בְּבֵיתֶךָ וּבְלֶכְתְּךָ בַדֶּרֶךְ
וּבְשָׁכְבְּךָ וּבְקוּמֶךָ וּקְשַׁרְתָּם לְאוֹת עַל יָדֶךָ וְהָיוּ לְטֹטָפֹת
בֵּין עֵינֶיךָ וּכְתַבְתָּם עַל מְזֻזוֹת בֵּיתֶךָ וּבִשְׁעָרֶיךָ
וְהָיָה אִם שָׁמֹעַ תִּשְׁמְעוּ אֶל מִצְוֺתַי אֲשֶׁר אָנֹכִי
מְצַוֶּה אֶתְכֶם הַיּוֹם לְאַהֲבָה אֶת יְהוָֹה אֱלֹהֵיכֶם וּלְעָבְדוֹ
בְּכָל לְבַבְכֶם וּבְכָל נַפְשְׁכֶם וְנָתַתִּי מְטַר אַרְצְכֶם בְּעִתּוֹ
יוֹרֶה וּמַלְקוֹשׁ וְאָסַפְתָּ דְגָנֶךָ וְתִירֹשְׁךָ וְיִצְהָרֶךָ וְנָתַתִּי
עֵשֶׂב בְּשָׂדְךָ לִבְהֶמְתֶּךָ וְאָכַלְתָּ וְשָׂבָעְתָּ הִשָּׁמְרוּ לָכֶם
פֶּן יִפְתֶּה לְבַבְכֶם וְסַרְתֶּם וַעֲבַדְתֶּם אֱלֹהִים אֲחֵרִים
וְהִשְׁתַּחֲוִיתֶם לָהֶם וְחָרָה אַף יְהוָֹה בָּכֶם וְעָצַר אֶת
הַשָּׁמַיִם וְלֹא יִהְיֶה מָטָר וְהָאֲדָמָה לֹא תִתֵּן אֶת יְבוּלָהּ
וַאֲבַדְתֶּם מְהֵרָה מֵעַל הָאָרֶץ הַטֹּבָה אֲשֶׁר יְהוָֹה נֹתֵן לָכֶם
וְשַׂמְתֶּם אֶת דְּבָרַי אֵלֶּה עַל לְבַבְכֶם וְעַל נַפְשְׁכֶם וּקְשַׁרְתֶּם
אֹתָם לְאוֹת עַל יֶדְכֶם וְהָיוּ לְטוֹטָפֹת בֵּין עֵינֵיכֶם וְלִמַּדְתֶּם
אֹתָם אֶת בְּנֵיכֶם לְדַבֵּר בָּם בְּשִׁבְתְּךָ בְּבֵיתֶךָ וּבְלֶכְתְּךָ
בַדֶּרֶךְ וּבְשָׁכְבְּךָ וּבְקוּמֶךָ וּכְתַבְתָּם עַל מְזֻזוֹת בֵּיתֶךָ
וּבִשְׁעָרֶיךָ לְמַעַן יִרְבּוּ יְמֵיכֶם וִימֵי בְנֵיכֶם עַל הָאֲדָמָה
אֲשֶׁר נִשְׁבַּע יְהוָֹה לַאֲבֹתֵיכֶם לָתֵת לָהֶם כִּימֵי הַשָּׁמַיִם
עַל הָאָרֶץ

Fig. 50. *Mezuzah.*

25:19): ". . . you shall blot out the memory of Amalek from under heaven. . . ." (The story of Amalek can be found in Exodus 17:8–16 and is reviewed in Deuteronomy 25:17–19.) Only in the Deuteronomy text is a reason given for such hatred of Amalek; the Exodus text just relates the event. However, Amalek has come down through many *midrashim* and many generations as a character (and people) of evil, with Haman being one of his principal descendants.

After crossing out Amalek, he states aloud: "I am writing this Torah (or *mezuzah*—the parchment placed on the doorpost as a symbol of the Torah and love for God being taught in that house—or *tefillin*—phylacteries worn about the head and arm as part of the weekday morning prayer; they serve as a reminder to love God and perform the commandments) for the sake of its holiness and for the sake of God's holiness." He then reads aloud the sentence to be written and writes it. Each time he is about to write the holy name of God he says: "I am writing the name of God for the sake of the holiness of The Name." (See figures 50 and 51.)

What is important in a *sofer*'s work is a principle called *kavvanah* [intention]. A *sofer* must clearly have the proper frame of mind when working on a work of holiness. He must *intend* to write what he writes. If the intention is not there—if, for example, he is sleepy, or he thinks of something else, or his mind wanders—the work he has done is considered invalid. Sincerity of purpose and pure dedication must accompany (and are part of) the spiritual activity of a *sofer*.

Of course, there are other restrictions involved in a *sofer*'s work, and other possibilities for invalidating work. For example, God's holy

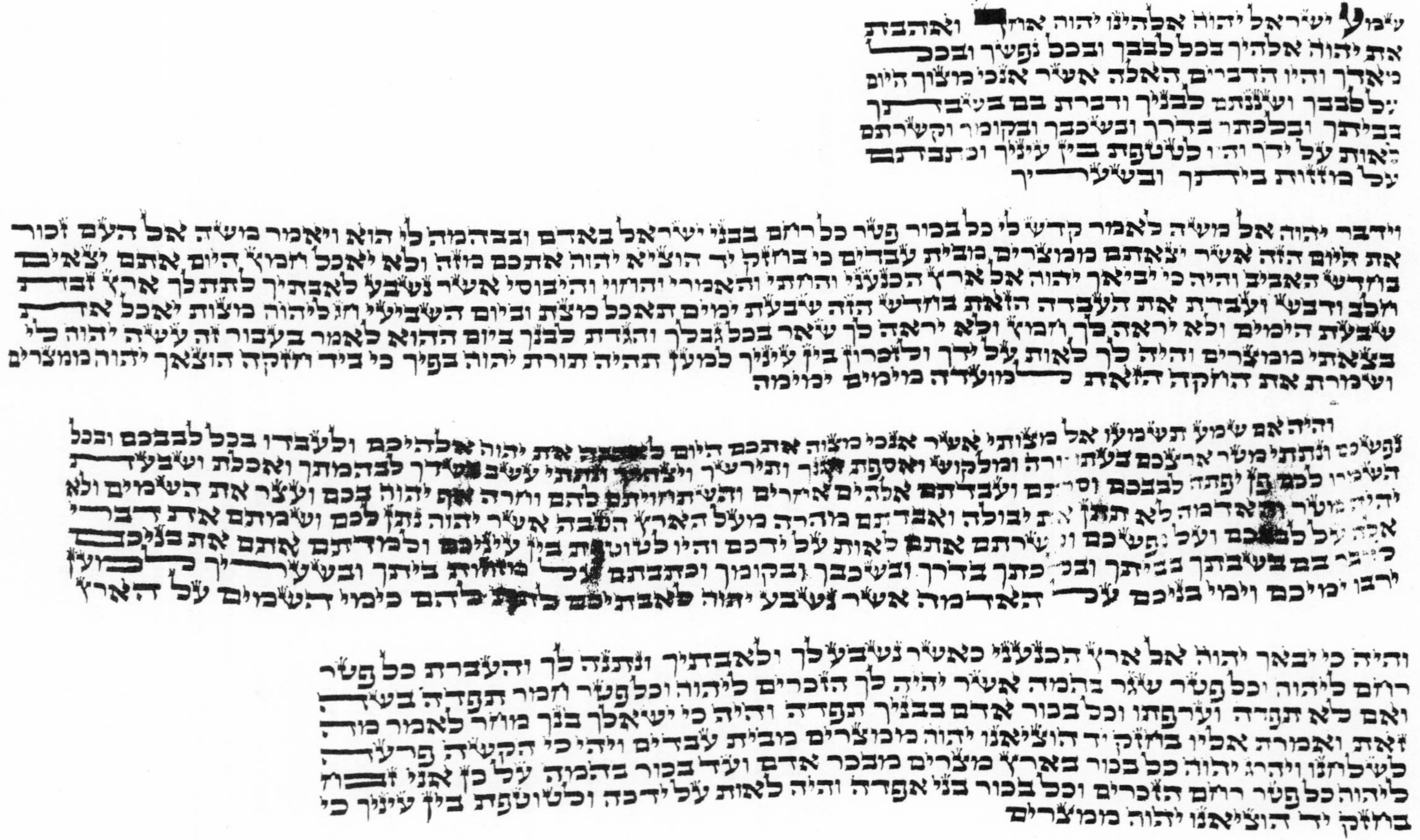

Fig. 51. *Tefillin*. These are the four pieces of parchment found inside the boxes.

name may not be erased (even though erasure of other errors is permitted). If the *sofer* makes an error in God's holy name, the entire piece of parchment he is working on must be set aside and later placed in a *genizah* (a burial ground, stone or chamber for unusable or invalid religious articles).

A *sofer* is called a סוֹפֵר סת״ם, a *sofer* STaM, which is an acronym for the three principal religious articles he produces: סֵפֶר תּוֹרָה (Sefer *torah*, a Torah scroll), תְּפִילִין (T*efillin*, phylacteries) and מְזוּזָה (M*ezuzah*). These three each have somewhat different requirements for their production: column width, what may be written from memory, what to do in case of error, and other details. Some examples of these requirements can be seen in the *mezuzah*. When the sofer writes the first line, he must enlarge two letters (ע and ד) so that it looks like this:

[Hear, O Israel, the Lord is our God, the Lord is one.] One reason for this is the following. Since א and ע sound alike, one might replace the *ayin* with an *alef*. This would change the pronunciation of

from *sh'ma* to *shema* and also change the meaning of the first line so that it would read: *"Perhaps,* Israel, the Lord is our God, the Lord is one."* The *ayin* is enlarged to prevent this from happening.

In the last word

since ד can often be visually confused with ר, one might write אַחֵר instead, and the line would read: "Hear, O Israel, Lord is our God, Lord is *another."* This implies that there are two Lords with the same name. So the ד is enlarged to leave no doubt. (Many Jews add special emphasis to these enlarged letters when saying them aloud during prayer as an additional reinforcement.)

Additionally, the two enlarged letters spell עֵד [witness], so that by saying this line, one attests to the uniqueness of God.

Another requirement in writing a *mezuzah* is seen on the reverse side. The *sofer* must write the word שׁדּי , *shaddai,* one of the names of God meaning "the Almighty." It can also be an acronym for

שׁוֹמֵר דְּלָתוֹת יִשְׂרָאֵל

[*shomer d'latot yisrael,* Guardian of the doors of Israel]. (This word appears on the outside of the *mezuzah* when it is rolled and placed in its holder on the doorpost.)

Finally, at the bottom of the reverse side, written upside down, are the words כוזו במוכסז כוזו which mean nothing. These letters stand for

יהוה אלהינו יהוה

[Lord, our God, Lord]. Each stands for the letter it follows in the alphabet— כ stands for י, ו stands for ה, ז for ו, and so on. God's holy names are considered too sacred to be written on the outside of the piece of parchment when also written on the inside. Hence, this substitution. (*Shaddai* is one of God's names, but not one of the *holy* names.)

A *sofer* also has special requirements concerning the tools and materials he may use. A common element is that all materials come from "organic" sources. The material he writes on, the parchment, must be made from the skin of a kosher animal, though the animal need not have been ritually slaughtered. (Most work is written on *klaf*—or parchment—made from sheepskin which has been soaked, bleached, pressed, and dried; though other skins such as calfskin (vellum), deerskin, etc., are permissible, as they all come from kosher animals.) When pieces of parchment have been completed in their writing (as in a *sefer torah*), the pieces are sewn together using *giddin,* thread made from the tendon tissue of the foot muscles of a kosher animal. The seams are reinforced with pieces of parchment glued to the back, and using a glue made from a kosher animal or a vegetable source. The sewn pieces are then bound onto two wooden poles, called *atzei ḥayyim* (trees of life, as the Torah is called a tree of life). The ink is a combination of ingredients to insure blackness and durability. Today most *sofrim* boil together gallnuts, gum arabic, and copper sulfate crystals. Each *sofer* has his own recipe that has been handed down for generations. Some add vinegar and alcohol.

A *sofer* uses a feather (also from a kosher animal) cut into the shape of a quill as his writing instrument. Goose or turkey feathers are usually used. Where a non-Jewish scribe will cut his quill with a square edge for broad lettering, a *sofer* will cut his quill with the nib at an angle (similar to that of an oblique, or left-handed, nib), because of the technical requirements of the Torah script, a standard script that has been the same for generations and which has certain exact require-

אבגדהוזח
טיכךלמםנן
סעפףצץק
רשת

צורת אותיות נוסח ספרד (וליש)

אבגדההוז
זטיכךרל
מםנןסעפ
ףצץקרשת

Fig. 52. Torah script, Ashkenazic (top) and Sephardic forms.

ments. (There are two versions, Ashkenazic and Sephardic—see figure 52.) A *sofer* will use his pen at various angles; he will change the angle of the nib as it moves; crowns, called *tagin,* must be added on certain letters, and these are formed by placing the quill on the very corner of the oblique nib. There are specific requirements as to the way to begin and end each individual letter. The letters hang only from a top line which has been scribed on the parchment.

Even from this brief description, it is possible to see what a remarkable role the *sofer* has played in the history of Jewish life and tradition. He is God's messenger for the words of God's Torah. It is the *sofer*'s task to keep the books of "the people of the book" accurate and pure. But he is also an integral person in the everyday life of the Jew, providing the religious articles necessary for the individual, the home, and the community. As a servant of the Word, he ties the people to God and God to the people.

One of the most wonderful aspects of the art of Hebrew calligraphy is the connection it offers us to our history. At any moment, as you practice a page of letters or work on an illuminated project, you can join in this unbroken line of tradition that extends from the first tablets carried in the ark of the Tabernacle down through all the past and present generations that have taken, and still take, those words to heart.

Selected Bibliography

GENERAL SOURCES, JEWISH

Encyclopaedia Judaica. The *EJ* (as it is abbreviated) is a rich resource for any information about Jewish life, history, and religion. It is comprehensive and all-encompassing. It also includes many varied entries on different areas of Jewish art.

GENERAL SOURCES ON JEWISH ART

These are good basic references that give an overview of the history of Jewish art.

Goodenough, Edwin R. *Jewish Symbols in the Greco-Roman Period.* 13 vols. Princeton: Princeton University Press, 1953–69.

Gutfeld, Ludwig. *Jewish Art from the Bible to Chagall.* New York: Thomas Yoseloff, 1968.

Gutmann, Joseph, ed. *Beauty in Holiness: Studies in Jewish Customs and Ceremonial Art.* New York: Ktav, 1970.

Katz, Karl, et al. *From the Beginning: Archeology and Art in the Israel Museum, Jerusalem.* New York: Morrow, 1968.

Landsberger, Franz. *A History of Jewish Art.* Cincinnati: UAHC, 1946.

Roth, Cecil. *Jewish Art: An Illustrated History.* New York: McGraw-Hill, 1961; rev. ed., Greenwich, Conn.: New York Graphic Society, 1971.

HISTORICAL AND BACKGROUND MATERIAL

"Calligraphy." *The New Encyclopaedia Brittanica.* 1970. Vol. III. This is a well-written, comprehensive summary of the development of calligraphy in various cultures and languages, from Hebrew and Aramaic, through the European, to the Chinese and Japanese.

"Hebrew Alphabet." *Encyclopaedia Judaica.* 1972. Vol. I. This discusses the historical development of Hebrew letters. A bit scholarly in places, but provides important information.

HEBREW CALLIGRAPHY AND ILLUMINATED MANUSCRIPTS

Cockerell, Sydney C. *Old Testament Miniatures.* New York: Braziller, 1969. One book in a series of large-format books featuring different periods or styles of illuminated manuscripts in each volume.

Davidovitch, David. *The Ketuba: Jewish Marriage Contracts through the Ages.* Tel Aviv: Lewin Epstein, 1968. A beautifully illustrated and richly informative volume that details the history of the Jewish marriage contract and the various artistic expressions it found among Jews in various places and periods.

Greenspan, Jay. "A Practical Guide to Hebrew Calligraphy." In *The Jewish Catalog.* Vol. I. Edited by Richard Siegel, Michael Strassfeld, and Sharon Strassfeld. Philadelphia: Jewish Publication Society, 1973. A preliminary and elementary discussion of the fundamentals of lettering.

Guttman, Joseph. *Hebrew Manuscript Painting.* New York: Braziller, 1978. Another in the Braziller series of large-format books. A good resource, even if some reproductions are not of the best quality.

Leaf, Reuben. *Hebrew Alphabets.* New York: Bloch Publishing Company, 1976. This book gives sample scripts from different historical periods of Hebrew lettering, as extrapolated from manuscripts. Hebrew typefaces are also included. An almost indispensable volume for the serious calligrapher.

Moss, David. "The Lovely Art of Ketubbah-making." In *The Jewish Catalog.* Vol. I. A concise, inspiring, useful, and informative guide for the beginning *ketubah* maker.

Narkiss, Bezalel. *Hebrew Illuminated Manuscripts.* New York: Macmillan, 1969. An indispensable volume that shows the historical and geographical development of Hebrew manuscripts. It is a companion piece to the Davidovitch book.

Rosenberg, Joel. "A Treatise on the Making of Letters." In *The Jewish Catalog.* Vol. I. A unique and evocative discussion of the spiritual and practical sides to Hebrew letters.

Toby, L. F. *The Art of Hebrew Lettering.* Tel Aviv: Cosmopolite, 1973. The only manual of scripts for Hebrew calligraphers. A companion piece to the Leaf book.

Other good resources are articles in the *EJ* on *ketuba, mizrah,* synagogue mosaics, Jewish art, etc. Also look at *haggadot* and *megillot* produced throughout the centuries as varieties of Jewish artistic expression.

GENERAL CALLIGRAPHY BOOKS AND SOURCES FOR ILLUMINATION

Child, Heather. *Calligraphy Today.* London: Studio Books, 1963. A book that profusely illustrates the state of the art of modern calligraphy.

Douglass, Ralph. *Calligraphic Lettering with Wide Pen and Brush.* 3rd rev. ed. New York: Watson-Guptill, 1967. Useful for its instructional format.

Fairbank, Alfred. *A Book of Scripts.* London: Faber and Faber, 1975. Another leading calligrapher.

Goudy, Frederic W. *The Alphabet and Elements of Lettering.* New York: Dover, 1963. An excellent book that details the history of letter development.

Johnston, Edward. *Writing & Illuminating & Lettering.* New York: Pentalic Corporation, 1977. This book is often called the Bible of modern calligraphers. Johnston was instrumental in reviving the art of lettering with a broad-nibbed pen around the turn of the twentieth century.

Lamb, C. M., ed. *The Calligrapher's Handbook.* New York: Pentalic Corporation, 1976. A manual for professionals and serious students. The companion book to Johnston's. Produced by the Society of Scribes and Illuminators, a prestigious organization of talented and superior calligraphers, based in England, with extremely high standards for membership.

Macdonald, Byron J. *Calligraphy: The Art of Lettering with the Broad Pen.* New York: Pentalic Corporation, 1966. A nicely designed and useful book.

Ogg, Oscar. *The 26 Letters.* New York: Thomas Y. Crowell, 1961. A good discussion of paleography—the initial development of letters.

Reynolds, Lloyd J. *Italic Calligraphy and Handwriting: Exercises and Text.* New York: Pentalic Corporation, 1969. A manual written by one of the leading forces of calligraphy in America. Reynolds was instrumental in introducing Italic as an alternative for learning handwriting in primary schools.

Svaren, Jacqueline. *Written Letters: 22 Alphabets for Calligraphers.* Freeport, Maine: Bond Wheelwright, 1975. A well-designed, comprehensive book that teaches historical hands.

The above list is not intended to be comprehensive, but only to give an overview of some valuable resources. Other resources to turn to include the dozens of Dover books that deal with a range of artistic wealth. Look at illuminated Bibles, Books of Hours, the *Book of Kells,* and other volumes in the Braziller series such as *Italian Renaissance Illuminations, Persian Painting, Celtic and Anglo-Saxon Painting,* and more. Finally, check your local libraries for books on watercolor techniques, painting, and drafting techniques.

THE SOFER AND HIS ART

These two articles are comprehensive and informative.

Kelman, Stuart. "The Calligraphy of the Classic Scribe." In *The Jewish Catalog.* Vol. I.

"Sofer." *Encyclopaedia Judaica.* 1972. Vol. XIV.

MIDRASHIC MATERIAL ON LETTERS

These books are not calligraphy books *per se,* but deal with the spiritual and symbolic side of Hebrew letters. They are enriching and exciting books. (A midrash is any sort of homiletical material, often using symbolism, metaphor, analogy, poetry, alliteration, onomatopoeia, and other literary devices to express a thought, often related to the Bible.)

Diringer, David. *The Story of the Aleph Bet.* New York: Thomas Yoseloff, 1960.

Kushner, Lawrence. (*Sefer Otiyot:*) *The Book of Letters: A Mystical Alef-bait.* New York: Harper and Row, 1975.

Podwal, Mark. *A Book of Hebrew Letters.* Philadelphia: Jewish Publication Society, 1978.

Shahn, Ben. *The Alphabet of Creation.* New York: Schocken Books, 1954.

———. *Love and Joy about Letters.* New York: Grossman Publishers, 1968.

Appendix A

Institutions as Resources

These institutions usually have books and illuminated manuscripts either on display or as part of their permanent collections. Such material provides invaluable aid to calligraphers and illuminators. Some institutions are open to the public, some require special permission for entry. It is wise to phone or write ahead concerning specific requirements. The list is not exhaustive, but rather eclectic.

MUSEUMS

Beth Hatefutsoth—Museum of the Jewish Diaspora. Tel Aviv University Campus. Tel Aviv, Israel.
B'nai Brith Klutznick Museum. Washington, D.C.
British Museum. London.
Israel Museum. Jerusalem.
Jewish Museum. New York City.
Judah L. Magnus Museum. Berkeley, California.
Maurice Spertus Museum. Chicago.
Museum of Typography. Safed, Israel.
Skirball Museum. Los Angeles.
Smithsonian Institution. Judaic Collection. Washington, D.C.
Tel-Aviv Museum. Tel Aviv, Israel.
The Vatican Museums. Rome.
Yeshiva University Museum. New York City.

LIBRARIES

Hebrew Union College Library. New York City.
Huntington Library. San Marino, California.
Jewish Theological Seminary Library. New York City.
Jewish National and University Library. Jerusalem.
Library of Congress. Washington, D.C.

Morgan Library. New York City.
New York Public Library. New York City.
Schocken Library. Jerusalem.
Trinity College. Dublin.
Vatican Library. Rome.
YIVO Library. New York City.

Appendix B

Calligraphic Societies

Calligraphy has increased greatly in popularity over the last two decades, and calligraphic societies have sprung up all over. These organizations are made up of people who support, promote, or simply enjoy calligraphy. Members of these groups are your best resource for support and information. The following list of calligraphic societies is taken from the *Calligraphy Quarterly,* published by the Society of Scribes in New York City, and is reproduced with the kind permission of that organization.

Association of Berkshire Calligraphers
c/o Jack Fitterer
RD 1, Rt. 23
Hillsdale, New York 12529

Calligraphy Guild of Pittsburgh
P.O. Box 8167
Pittsburgh, Pennsylvania 15217

Calligraphers Guild
Box 304
Ashland, Oregon 97520

Calligraphy Workshop
14940 Beech Daly Road
Redford, Michigan 48240

Capitol Calligraphers
3589 Pringle Road S.E.
Salem, Oregon 97302

Chautauqua Calligraphers' Guild
c/o L. Sherman Brooks
Rural Box 321, RFD 2, St. Rt. 380
Jamestown, New York 14701

Chicago Calligraphy Collective
P.O. Box 11333
Chicago, Illinois 60611

Colleagues of Calligraphy
P.O. Box 4024
St. Paul, Minnesota 55104

Colorado Calligraphers Guild
Box 6413
Cherry Creek Station
Denver, Colorado 80206

Connecticut Calligraphy Society
P.O. Box 493
New Canaan, Connecticut 06854

Escribiente
P.O. Drawer 26718
Albuquerque, New Mexico 87125

Friends of Calligraphy
P.O. Box 5194
San Francisco, California 94101

Goose Quill Guild
c/o Allen Q. Wong
Department of Art
Oregon State University
Corvallis, Oregon 97331

Handwriters Guild of Toronto
60 Logandale Road
Willowdale, Ontario CANADA

Indiana Guild of Calligraphers
1712 E. 86th Street
Indianapolis, Indiana 46240

Indiana Calligrapher's Association
Route 3, Box 192
Floyds Knobs, Indiana 47119

Indiana Calligrapher's Association
2501 Pamela Drive
New Albany, Indiana 47150

Island Scribes
c/o Janice Glander-Bandyk
1000 East 98th Street
Brooklyn, New York 11236

Lettering Arts Guild of Boston
80 Chestnut Street, No. 3
Brookline, Massachusetts 02146

**Mensa's Calligraphy
Special Interest Group**
c/o Sally Jackson
2405 Medford Court East
Fort Worth, Texas 76109

Michigan Association of Calligraphers
25842 Glover Court
Farmington Hills, Michigan 48018

New Orleans Calligraphers Association
6161 Marquette Place
New Orleans, Louisiana 70118

Opulent Order of Practicing Scribes
c/o Alice Girand
1310 West 7th Street
Roswell, New Mexico 88201

Philadelphia Calligrapher's Society
P.O. Box 7174
Elkins Park, Pennsylvania 19117

Phoenix Society for Calligraphy
1709 North 7th Street
Phoenix, Arizona 85006

Society for Calligraphy
P.O. Box 64174
Los Angeles, California 90064

Society for Calligraphy and Handwriting
c/o The Factory of Visual Art
4649 Sunnyside North
Seattle, Washington 98103

Society for Italic Handwriting
British Columbia Branch
P.O. Box 48390
Bentall Centre
Vancouver, British Columbia
V7X 1A2 CANADA

Society for Italic Handwriting
69 Arlington Road
London, N.W. 1 ENGLAND

Society of Scribes and Illuminators
c/o Federation of British Craft Societies
43 Earlham Street
London WC2 ENGLAND

The Fairbank Society
1970 Fairfield Place
Victoria, BC
V8S 4J4 CANADA

The Friends for Calligraphy
1804 Sonoma
Berkeley, California 94797

**The International Association of Master
Penmen and Teachers of Handwriting**
2213 Arlington Avenue
Middletown, Ohio 45042

The League of Hand Binders
7513 Melrose Avenue
Los Angeles, California 90046

**The Michigan Association
of Calligraphers**
c/o Susanne Ebel
25842 Glover Court
Farmington, Michigan 48018

The New Haven Calligraphers Guild
c/o Jay C. Rochelle
27 High Street
New Haven, Connecticut 06510

Tidewater Calligraphy Guild
c/o Michael R. Sull
220 Cortland Lane
Virginia Beach, Virginia 23452

Society of Scribes
P.O. Box 933
New York, New York 10022

San Antonio Calligrapher's Guild
2407 Shadow Cliff
San Antonio, Texas 78232

Valley Calligraphy Guild
3241 Kevington
Eugene, Oregon 97405

Vereniging Mercator
Gaasterlandstraat 96
Haarlem, HOLLAND

Washington Calligrapher's Guild
Box 23818
Washington, DC 20024

**Western American Branch of the
Society for Italic Handwriting**
c/o Mrs. Jo Ann DiSciullo
6800 S.E. 32nd Avenue
Portland, Oregon 97202

Write On Calligraphers
No. 5, 7929 196th S.W.
Edmonds, Washington 98020

Appendix C
Examples of
Illuminated Manuscripts

באחד בשבת
בחמשה עשר יום לחדש אלול שנת
חמשת אלפים ושבע מאות ושלשים ושמונה לבריאת
עולם למנין שאנו מונין כאן פילדסטון שבברונקס ניו יורק במדינת
אמריקה הצפונית איך החתן ברוך צדיק בר יצחק עמנואל וציפה שרה
למשפחת לוסטבדר אמר לה להדא בתולתא רחל חנה בת משה ומרים למשפחת
אוסטוב הוי לי לאנתו כדת משה וישראל ואנא אפלח ואוקיר ואיזון ואפרנס יתיכי ליכי
כהלכות גוברין יהודאין דפלחין ומוקרין וזנין ומפרנסין לנשיהון בקושטא ויהיבנא ליכי מוהר
בתוליכי כסף זוזי מאתן דחזי ליכי מדאורייתא ומזוניכי וכסותיכי וספוקיכי ומיעל לותיכי כאורח
כל ארעא וצביאת מרת רחל חנה בתולתא דא והות ליה לאנתו ודין נדוניא דהנעלת ליה מבי אבוה
בין בכסף בין בדהב בין בתכשיטין במאני דלבושא בשימושי דירה ובשימושי דערסא הכל קבל עליו
ברוך צדיק חתן דנן במאה זקוקים כסף צרוף וצבי ברוך צדיק חתן דנן והוסיף לה מן דיליה עוד מאה
זקוקים כסף צרוף אחרים כנגדן סך הכל מאתים זקוקים כסף צרוף וכך אמר ברוך צדיק חתן דנן אחריות
שטר כתובתא דא נדוניא דין ותוספתא דא קבלית עלי ועל ירתי בתראי להתפרע מן כל שפר ארג נכסין וקנינין
דאית לי תחות כל שמיא דקנאי ודעתיד אנא למקנא נכסין דאית להון אחריות ודלית להון אחריות כלהון
יהון אחראין וערבאין לפרוע מנהון שטר כתובתא דא נדוניא דין ותוספתא דא מנאי ואפילו מן גלימא דעל
כתפאי בחיי ובמותי מן יומא דנן ולעלם ואחריות וחומר שטר כתובתא דא נדוניא דין ותוספתא דא קבל עליו
ברוך צדיק חתן דנן כחומר כל שטרי כתובות ותוספתות דנהגין בבנות ישראל העשויין כתקון חכמינו זכרונם לברכה
וצבו מר ברוך צדיק בר יצחק עמנואל וציפה שרה חתן דנן ומרת רחל חנה בת משה ומרים בתולתא דא
למשבק דין לדא ודא לדין למנהג כל יומי חייהון באורחא דאורייתא כהלכות גוברין יהודאין וצבו
ברעות נפשיהון ואסכימו לקבלא על נפשיהון בית דינא דכנישתא דרבנן ודבית מדרשא
דרבנן דארעתא דקיימא או מאן דאתי מן חילה היך רשו יחידאה לאלפא יתהון למיזל באורחא
דאורייתא ולמרחם ולאוקרא דין לדא ודא לדין כל יומי מיגד נישואיהון וקבילו על
נפשיהון כל חד מנהון לארשאה לחבריה לזמנא יתה לבי דינא דאידכר מן עילא אן
יתרמא תגרא בניהון בדיל דיכול למיהוי כל חד דירעי מנהון בדיני דאורייתא
כל יומי חיוהי וארשו לבי דינא דאידכר למרמא פיצויין על כל חד מנהון אן לא יצבי
למיזל קדמוהי בדינא או אן לא יצבי לצייתא לפסקא דדיניה דלא כאסמכתא
ודלא כטופסי דשטרי וקנינא מן ברוך צדיק בר יצחק עמנואל וציפה
שרה חתן דנן למרת רחל חנה בת משה ומרים בתולתא דא ומן מרת
רחל חנה בת משה ומרים בתולתא דא למר ברוך צדיק בר
יצחק עמנואל וציפה שרה חתן דנן על כל מה דכתוב ומפורש
לעיל במנא דכשר למקניא ביה והכל שריר וקים

נאום   עד

נאום   עד

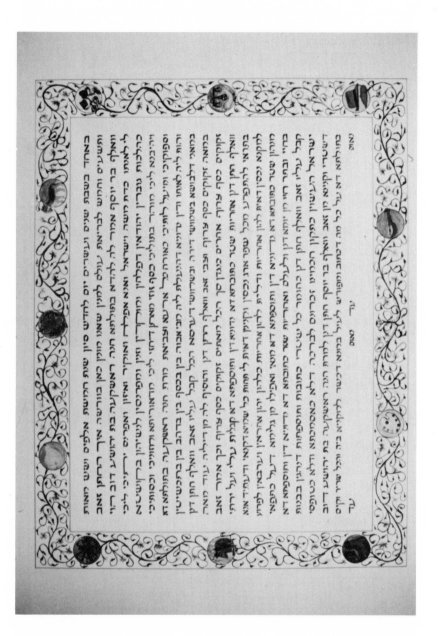

שׁיר הַמַּעֲלוֹת לְדָוִד
הִנֵּה מַה טּוֹב וּמַה נָּעִים
שֶׁבֶת אַחִים גַּם יָחַד
כַּשֶּׁמֶן הַטּוֹב עַל הָרֹאשׁ
יֹרֵד עַל הַזָּקָן זְקַן אַהֲרֹן
שֶׁיֹּרֵד עַל פִּי מִדּוֹתָיו
כְּטַל חֶרְמוֹן שֶׁיֹּרֵד עַל הַרְרֵי צִיּוֹן
כִּי שָׁם צִוָּה יְהוָה אֶת הַבְּרָכָה
חַיִּים עַד עוֹלָם

Index

INDEX

INDEX